CW00469895

Gobsmacked is a l
extraordinary
A rec
Matt Bi

*In these pages, Kevin has wonderfully revealed his love
for both the Lord and for the people of Mitcham.
I look forward to the next edition*
George Banks, ex-Boys Brigade Captain

*Every life tells a story and Kevin's book is an honest,
poignant and, at times, funny ringside seat to his life story.
He shares the highs and lows, the stuff he got right and
the stuff he got wrong, the opportunities seized, and the
lessons learnt. There are some real gems of wisdom that
speak through the pages! Above all, his story reminds
us that life is to be lived and that the best stories
are when we invite God in!*
Andy Frost, author of Long Story Short

*As I have read this real-life story of the journey of one
"below average" man, I remain utterly "Gobsmacked" at
the way the incredible grace and favour of God has
been upon Kev and Jane's lives, and the ways in which
they just do life. This life, of course, is focused so much
on serving others and helping them to experience
the love of God which is found in Jesus!*
Pastor Jonathon Dyke, Kingdom Faith Church

Whether you know Kevin or not, this snapshot of his journey in life will bring a smile to your face, a tear to your eye, and probably moments of disbelief as you read of antics that "may have gone too far"! Kevin's vulnerability in writing makes this book easy to read, heart-warming, humorous, and yet in places, deeply challenging, as we read of a faith that underpins life itself.
Martin Durham, Director of K180

This book skips through Kevin's life, signposting us to his values, his loves, and his hopes. It is a positive and humorous reflection of one man's journey, framed by the context of all that drives him: his Christian faith and his love for people.
Celia Dawson, Headteacher,
Cricket Green School, Mitcham

A few years ago, Kevin and Jane introduced me to the term "Gobsmacked" – one of the words that didn't make the journey from the mother country to the colonies! In this book, my friend, Kevin, opens his life and shares many of the times he's been 'gobsmacked' by God. The extraordinary truth is how ordinary Kevin and Jane's lives have been. And that's precisely the genius of this book.
Phil Tuttle, President & CEO
Walk Thru the Bible Ministries, Atlanta, GA USA

This book takes you on an adventure, chronicling the strong affirmation of God's calling on one man's life and how this results in radical change. It reminds us of our own calling from God, that we, too, are on a journey, and that God is keeping us and doing things in our lives. Every Christian will resonate with the encounter in this book.
Les Isaac OBE, President Ascension Trust

As you will read in this book, Kevin is a man of integrity as well as passion. He has extraordinary faith and is a great encourager, full of mischief, but most of all, a real man after God's heart. He is authentic!
Gail Millar, former General Manager of Torch Holiday and Retreat Centre for people with sight loss

I've known Kevin Vickers for about 20 years now. We inhabit different circles: I live for political solutions, he lives for those that faith can bring, and our worlds intersect at Cricket Green School where we're both privileged to govern. Kevin is a quiet, measured man of absolute certainty, my opposite in many ways, but when he speaks, I always listen. This little book starts to tell you why. It tells you how and why a man of great humility can nevertheless be at the centre of things, and can make things happen. It tells you, gently and humorously, of his childhood, his family, his career, his travels, and, most of all, his faith. It leaves you wanting more. I hope you enjoy it as much as I did.
Nick Draper, former Mayor of the London Borough of Merton

Kevin, more than most, understood that a business is not simply a viable commercial concept, but vital to it are the people behind it. His deep and genuine interest in the people not just the commerce was a major strength. For someone who treads lightly, Kevin leaves a large footprint, and it is my privilege that our paths should have crossed, albeit briefly, some twenty years ago.
Mel Rooke, former Chief Executive, Croydon Business Venture Ltd

GOBSMACKED!

Issachar Global Publishing

PO Box 38082

London

SW19 1YQ

UK

www.issacharglobal.com

Thanks to

A massive thanks to **Matt Bird** for leading the Writing My Book course that taught me how to write this book. Through his counsel, instruction and guidance, I was motivated and mobilised to do something I never, ever thought I'd do.

Special thanks to **Paul Lansley**, my fishing buddy for his amazing illustrations - the front cover and the seven subsections of this book. Paul, you have an incredible gift and skill, and I am really grateful for the time and effort you've taken to put these together. You're not a bad fisherman either!

My biggest thanks must go to my wife **Jane,** who encouraged me to join the course in the first place. She has listened to me read out loud every word and paragraph, constantly interrupting her television programmes for two months. She is probably the real author of this book, and I would like to dedicate *Gobsmacked* to Jane.

KEVIN VICKERS

Contents

Gobsmacked in my Family

Gobsmacked at Church

Introduction

My wife, Jane, said she was *Gobsmacked* when an unexpected visitor turned up at the hospital in the USA following our youngest son's accident. Since then, we've been using that phrase a lot. It can mean, *amazed or utterly astonished*. It can also be a *wow* or defining moment in our life; or a wake-up call like a smack in the mouth. A time to stop and reflect, look back and be thankful. An opportunity to be amazed at how one thing has led to the next. And a moment to make intentional plans for the future.

That's what this book is about. Gobsmacked is my first attempt at storytelling my way through my own life's ups and downs, successes and failures, good times, bad times, and sometimes crazy and funny adventures that have turned out okay in the end!

I sincerely hope that this collection of honest and poignant stories will warm your heart to see your own life journey in a fresh new light, and perhaps you too will be *Gobsmacked* or amazed at how things can turn out!

KEVIN VICKERS

Sure and steadfast

GOBSMACKED
IN MY EARLY YEARS

KEVIN VICKERS

Chapter 1
A Good Start in Life

My Dad was a postman with the Royal Mail. In the earlier days, he would walk the streets of Clapham delivering letters, but later would work in the London Sorting Office at King Edward Buildings, Newgate Street. He loved his job; it was like his life, and as I've heard someone else speaking about their dad in a similar way, my dad delivered and sorted letters as if he'd been appointed personally by the Queen. He never taught me science or maths, but he taught me how to get the best shine on my shoes, and that it was important to polish them underneath too. He taught me many things without teaching me.

Looking back years later, I realise just how much I have learnt from my dad that I didn't know I was learning at the time. It has made me feel so grateful and appreciative for his presence and influence in my life. I wish I'd been able to tell him that.

Every week, he would shine the brass badges on his uniform and cap with *Brasso*. He took such pride in wearing his uniform and continued wearing his cap when it became less fashionable to do so. He wasn't into fashion, and he was a stickler for routine and habits. He used to say, *"Never cast a clout till May's out"*, and would religiously wait for June before discarding his vest and bringing out his summer clothes from the wardrobe.

We would buy him clothes for birthdays and Christmases, but before opening a new shirt he'd make sure his old shirts had totally worn out. One Christmas, my brother Mike and I decided to go through his wardrobe. We found unopened shirts...loads of them. So, we wrapped them up again and put them under the Christmas tree. We put tags on them saying things like, *"To Dad, from Marks and Spencer"*. M&S was one of his favourite shops, and still is my mum's today.

He taught me how to manage my money when I saw the *Golden Virginia* tins stacked in a pile at the bottom of his wardrobe, each with a sticker on it: *council tax, housekeeping, holiday, gas, electric...* When he got paid dad and mum would budget their money to pay the bills. They spent what they had and not what they didn't, and we never went without.

Dad would be paid in cash in those days and never had his own bank account. He was also a worrier: he worried about money but didn't need to. After he died in 1988, we found money hidden away in his wardrobe, money that he had put away for a "rainy day".

Mum worked at *Woolworth's* in Mitcham. Her claim to fame, which she still reminds us of, is that she was the youngest staff supervisor in the whole of London at the age of nineteen. Her manager was Mr Inkpen, who apparently was not very good at adding up, so would call Mum to help.

Dad worked long hours, so it was mum who looked after my brother and I most of the time. Unlike many other families, life at home was good: loving, secure and happy.

Mum made sure we always had what we needed and often spoilt us. She was, and still is, the typical homemaker of that past era: hardworking, selfless, giving, and the best mum for her boys.

We have never been very good at outward displays of affection; we don't hug a lot or say "I love you" much, but we are deeply close and show it in other ways. I think we get this from my Mum. My own family have learnt to be a bit more open with showing affection.

Mum's dad, Grandad who we called Addy, lived at home with us. Mike and I shared a bedroom with him and looking back I wonder whether he was where we get some of our craziness from. He would give funny names to the neighbours and throw water from the upstairs window.

Once, he put the hose on the "Effing-Graves", our next-door neighbours. On another occasion, he set his hair on fire lighting his cigarette. He would also have ridiculous sayings that I have since passed on to my children, and even now will come out when I am talking to others.

Solomon wrote many years ago in the Psalms that children are like arrows in a quiver, and that parents get the job of firing or releasing them from their bow towards the target. As I look back and reflect with immense gratitude, I am so grateful at the way Dad and Mum aimed me in the right direction and gave both myself and my brother a great start in life.

KEVIN VICKERS

Chapter 2
Fishing Stories

Mr Pavitt taught me to fish when I was about thirteen. He was a little man with a wide grin and a passion for freshwater fishing that he passed onto me. He and his wife were friends of my Mum. He would take me to stretches of private water on the River Wey where he was a member, and we would catch chub using a swim-feeder filled with maggots.

I have never forgotten that first experience, the exhilaration of hooking a big fish and learning to play it and reel it in. I still get that same feeling now when I get a bite and strike the rod. If the fish is hooked, the line goes tight, the rod bends, and the fight is on to land it successfully.

Mr Pavitt took my brother Mike with us once, only once. In fact, that might have been the last time he took me too. I was a bit older then, and Mike, who is five years younger than me, came for the first time. We fished the River Thames at Walton, and I remember climbing up the steep bank with a drop to the water line. We were setting up the rods when Mike accidentally kicked Mr Pavitt's landing net into the deep water, and it disappeared forever below the surface.

I immediately started to laugh, and so did Mike...we couldn't help ourselves. It was totally inappropriate, but it looked so funny. Mr Pavitt was not happy, and he told us so.

After that, Mike and I found ourselves snatching glances and finding it almost impossible to hold it together. I think that was my last trip with my fishing mentor, but I will always be grateful for his investment in my young life.

As a teenager, I would fish the River Mole under the railway bridge at Hampton Court. I'd go by the 152 bus from Mitcham or catch the number 30 train from Wimbledon. Sometimes, I'd take Mike and I remember on one occasion he caught his fingers in my wooden fold-up chair. It was so bad that a man fishing nearby took him to the hospital whilst I carried on fishing. He will never let me forget that. Thank God the man brought him back okay! What was I thinking?

I was fishing on the day my Dad died. I was twenty-seven now, married with our first son, who was five months old. It happened on his way to work that morning when he stood on the platform at Colliers Wood underground station waiting, as usual, for the first train to arrive at 5.30am. Dad had a massive heart attack and never recovered from it. I got to hear when I returned later that afternoon. He had died early morning and I had been fishing all day. I can't recall now how exactly I was told, but do remember experiencing a complete numbness at the devastating news that surely couldn't be true.

My Dad died the day before his 60th birthday, when he would have been entitled to his pension. His work colleagues honoured him and paid tribute to his quiet and conscientious nature, and a red postal van formed part of the funeral procession. My Mum put an advertisement in the local newspaper for information, but no one responded.

Later, I would sometimes drive to Colliers Wood station at night, park up and wait. Watching in my rear-view mirror, hoping, and praying that my Dad would come out of the station so I could drive him home like I used to do. I wanted to see his overused Marks and Spencer carrier bag with the white plastic handles under his arm. I wanted to see, again, the spring in his step that we now call the 'Vickers Bounce'. I wanted to smell that Dad aroma that only he carried.

When visiting Mum, I would find comfort in opening his side of the wardrobe and experience the familiar smell that I associated with him. It helped. I guess all these things helped, but grief is a process and a journey towards coming to terms with deep sadness, pain and loss in our lives. My growing experience is that, if we allow him, God will comfort and lead us through our grief to a place of trust and hope. I found that place.

I now realise why I gave up fishing when my Dad died.

It would be later in life, after my children had grown, that my passion for fishing would return. Perhaps I was now ready to let something go. Mr Pavitt was still around but we had lost contact. I'd sometimes drive past his house and see him carrying his rods to the car; fond memories come to mind. He sadly died recently.

I'm still fishing and I'm loving it. I don't take my brother anymore, but I have got a fishing buddy and we laugh a lot together – sometimes inappropriately!

I have also inherited the 'Vickers Bounce' from my dad, and passed it on to my youngest son Jon.

KEVIN VICKERS

Chapter 3
Boys Brigade

At the age of ten, I joined the 8th Kingston and Merton Boys Brigade. My Dad used to be in the 92nd London Company in Streatham, and twice a year we would visit. He would take me to their annual display, where I would watch the Boys showcase their marching formations, band and gymnastics. I loved it, particularly the band.

I wanted to play the bugle and belong to something as exciting and vibrant as this. I wanted to wear that uniform too! The other occasion was the 'Old Boys Bible Class' always on a cold autumn Sunday morning. Dad would be welcomed by the other past members, and I would remember familiar faces from previous years. I felt good about being there. Afterwards, we would always go to 'Tall Peter's' house. He lived around the corner with his wife a small round lady who would serve a roast beef dinner.

The BB would lay strong foundations in my life, like discipline, self-respect, leadership, responsibility and how to be organised. I was fiercely competitive and wanted to be the best I could at drill, gymnastics and particularly playing the bugle. I was so excited about getting my first bugle. It was a dented, old thing, but I practiced often, learnt quickly and soon was playing bugle calls before the others in my group. Over time, I would become solo bugler for our band.

On Remembrance Sunday, we would join the Sea Cadets and all the war veterans from the Royal British Legion, in Mitcham, for the parade to the cenotaph, where a small group of us buglers would have the honour of playing the Last Post and Naval Reveille.

When I was sixteen years old, I won the All-London Individual Buglers Competition; at the same time our band won the London District Competition. That year, we had the privilege of performing at the Royal Albert Hall in front of all the other Boys Brigade Companies across the UK. I got my photograph in the local newspaper playing the silver bugle.

My desire to be the best was sometimes at the expense of others. To get the annual 'perfect record' prize I had to attend on time: every Friday night meeting and Sunday morning Bible class during the BB year. This was so important for me that I would attend even if I was sick.

On one occasion when I was not well, my Mum pushed me to a meeting in a wheelchair, just to get my mark, and then pushed me home again. I remember feeling secretly smug and pleased when another boy, who I considered my rival, missed a meeting.

Like my Dad I would thoroughly clean the brass on my belt, my haversack, and my bugle with Brasso. You could see your face in them! I'd get the best possible shine on my black shoes too. For inspection at drill nights, I had to get 10/10, and most of the time I did.

I loved BB camp every year, travelling to Hampshire in the open back of a Luton van with all our kit bags, tents and equipment, waving at traffic and doing what boys do, before the onset of more stringent health and safety rules. Each day would revolve around bugle calls, like Reveille, to wake us up, Retreat, when the flag was lowered over the camp, and Lights Out, when we had to go to sleep. We'd do things like canoeing, mud walking, competitive games, midnight hikes and, before bed, we would all gather in the marquee for hot chocolate, prayers and sing the *Vesper* together.

I wasn't as good as I wanted to be at some of the more practical things; and still am not. I struggled as a tent commander pitching and striking our bell tent and setting up camp. I could never seem to fit the tent in its bag in time. Anthony Rowbottom was always so much better at this than me. That was a competition I never won!

I wasn't a Christian during these times. Mum and Dad didn't go to Church, but they sent me to Sunday school earlier on. Mr Coatman was my first Sunday school teacher; he was a tall man with white hair and a pronounced stutter. I liked him because he seemed to really care for us in his class. Mr West was my Boys Brigade Captain, a smart, strict man but with a kind heart. He would also lead the Bible Class on a Sunday morning.

It was during these times that the seeds were sown for my later faith to grow.

KEVIN VICKERS

Chapter 4
Aunty Brenda and Uncle Roy

Everyone probably has had an Auntie Brenda and Uncle Roy somewhere in their lives — people who always seemed to be there and were taken for granted at the time. Formative in my growing up, demonstrating unconditional love, kindness, forgiveness and grace, and helping to shape some of the practices and traditions I've adopted in my own family.

Mine came from my Dad's side of the family: Brenda was Dad's younger sister. They had a daughter, Carole, who is the same age as me, and we grew up together. Mum, apparently, was Brenda's supervisor at Woolworth's, they became friends, and that is how Mum and Dad came to meet.

Brenda had TB when she was thirteen and her life expectancy without an operation was to live up to her 21st birthday. Her parents courageously made the difficult decision to have the damaged lung removed, knowing that she was the thirteenth child to have this operation. The other twelve had all died!

Brenda survived but spent a year in hospital recovering, followed by a further time in a convalescent home on a farm where she was taught to smoke to calm her nerves! She used to say, "Lucky thirteen!"

Roy worked as the park keeper in Ravensbury Park where we used to go as kids. He used to tell us farfetched stories of how he looped the loop under Brighton pier in a Tiger Moth, only to be scolded by Brenda for massively exaggerating or making things up that never actually happened.

We would tease Uncle Roy badly. Mike and I would stick signs or funny pictures on his little cart that he drove around the park, and then we'd hide and watch. As families we sometimes went on holidays together and these were always fun. They were opportunities to do crazy things for a laugh. My Mum used to say I didn't know when to stop, and she was right. She still is! I am still prone at times to go that little bit too far. I remember we went to Devon and stayed at a holiday camp. I used to pin pegs on the back of Uncle Roy's coat without him knowing. Once, I attached a matchbox to a bit of cotton and safety-pinned it to the back of his jacket, so it swung from side to side when he walked along. They had a dog called Sandy that didn't like walking. I have a photograph somewhere of Uncle Roy carrying the dog over his shoulder with a yellow frisbee in its mouth. Funny times.

They lived in Glebe Court and sometimes after school I'd go straight to their flat for tea – not a cup of tea but 'dinner tea'. My favourite was the sliced beef in gravy, a kind of ready meal that was popular in the late 60s. I also loved eating thick chunks of cucumber. Since I was a baby and sick once, I've never drunk milk on its own. I also don't do butter or margarine.

This can be embarrassing because, back then all sandwiches, were made with butter, and everyone expected you to have milk on your cornflakes. I hated having to explain to people, and then them having to make a special plate just for me. At camp, I was the noisiest person eating cornflakes and always the last to finish! I never had that problem when I visited Auntie Brenda because she always knew.

I used to think that Auntie Brenda was the best-known person in Mitcham. It was like she talked to everyone. She would take ages to do her shopping and always had time for people. Spontaneously generous, she would literally give her last penny away. Like my Dad, her memory was amazing. She would be the first to telephone us on our birthdays, without fail. She would kiss us with her red lipstick and then lick her handkerchief with her mouth and wipe the mark away. Not my favourite memory!

When they moved to Ripley Court, on the Phipps Bridge Estate, I once found an old chair by the chute that someone was throwing away. I managed to sneak the chair into Auntie Brenda's front room when she wasn't looking. On another occasion, thinking it was funny, I let a stink bomb off in their flat that ended up ruining their new carpet. She was always so forgiving and would laugh it off.

I am so grateful that my three children also had Auntie Brenda and Uncle Roy in their lives. Our family is all the richer because of them. Uncle Roy became a Christian at my Dad's funeral. Something that was said touched his heart and caused him to respond to the message of Christ in a very personal way.

He'd still rattle his false teeth at us and move them around in his mouth, but Uncle Roy had found a new peace, purpose and hope in his life. Auntie Brenda would follow suit a bit later and would attend the Discovery Bible Study Group, which I would lead at the luncheon centre where she went.

I had the honour and privilege of conducting their funerals, pausing to reflect how lucky I was and grateful I am that I had an Auntie Brenda and Uncle Roy in my life and family.

I hope you had that, too.

Chapter 5

Being About Average at School

I had a crush on Miss Fisher at my first school, and persuaded Mum to take me to her wedding. We didn't go inside the church, but stood at a distance and watched as she came out all newly married. She was now Mrs Wood. I remember saying, she used to be a Kingfisher, but now she's a Woodpecker. I was quiet and shy at school and whilst I could be a practical joker at home, at school I went unnoticed. Mark Tanner, Les Roy and Stephen Gould were in my class, and we all started on the same day, aged five.

In the playground, we ran around pretending to be The Impossibles: crimefighters with superpowers. We played marbles on the drains and penny up the wall when the teachers weren't looking. In September, always around Mum's birthday week, Dad would take me 'conkering' to Bunce's Meadow in Morden Park. We would collect hundreds of them, and I would keep them in a big green cloth bag under my bed.

I loved playing conkers at school. Sometimes, we would soak them in vinegar and bake them in the oven so they would be harder and then you had more chance of winning. If you managed to break your opponent's conker and knock it off his string you were the winner, and your conker would be a 'one-er'. You'd keep adding the numbers on the more you won.

I got really good at catching a tennis ball and dodging when we were playing 'He'. Mark Tanner was the best and we became close friends and always sat together. This would continue right through to high school. Academically, I was about average but never the brightest in the class. I liked maths and spelling but struggled with my English and comprehension. I hated art, struggled with woodwork and metal work, and would come out in hot sweats whenever we did technical drawing. I wish I'd paid more attention in history and geography because they interest me now. Looking back, I was OK at classwork, but generally did not do so well in exams.

At middle school, I wanted to be in the football team but never quite made it. I got into the squad but was never picked for the team. I did get in once but that was the day I forgot to take my kit to school, so I couldn't play anyway.

I dreaded P.E. when the teachers chose two boys (it was usually boys), to be captains and they would pick teams. I can remember thinking, "Please don't pick me last!" I wasn't usually last, but never one of the first to be chosen. My friend, Les, who has learning difficulties would often be last.

I always wanted to work in a bank. I decided that would be my job when I left school, and it was. I needed to get four O Levels to be accepted but only managed one (maths). I got a CSE equivalent in biology and failed my English miserably. They took me on pending re-sitting English, which I did by attending evening classes at Merton College. I failed twice more and eventually passed with a grade C on my fourth attempt. That was such a painful time.

One of the things I learnt at school was that people get valued for what they can do, how good they are at something and how popular they are. This wasn't consciously taught but somehow it was implied and, at times, reinforced. It has taken me years to unlearn that lesson because it is just not true. I am passionate about reinforcing the truth, that everyone is special, valued, significant and full of possibilities. Life is precious, and none of us should be defined by our limitations.

I've lost contact with Mark Tanner, but Stephen Gould came round my house recently and I helped him apply for his 60+ Oyster travel card. I did the same for Les just after his birthday. Steve still has all our old class photographs from when we first started school all those years ago.

We both agreed to book a curry night, call Les and share memories together.

KEVIN VICKERS

Chapter 6
My Life-Changing Experience

I've always believed in God, but I have not always been a Christian. Like most people I talk to, I used to think a Christian was someone who did good, but now I know that's not true. Well, hopefully it is true on one level, but no one becomes a Christian by being good, doing good, or working hard.

I used to go to church twice on Sundays, but not for the right reasons. I'd go to BB Bible class to qualify for my 'perfect record' and some of us older boys would go to the evening service because the girls from the Girls Brigade went. We'd endure the one-hour service by sitting at the back and messing about shielded by the heads and hats of the older women in front, but looking forward to the after-meeting where the boys and girls got to meet in the lounge.

Faith was being sown in my young mind and heart without me realising it. The old hymns and choruses would return to my memory one day with richer and deeper meaning.

In Bible class, Dick, who was one of the officers would read a chapter from a book called Sergei. Sergei was in the secret police in the old Soviet Union and led vicious attacks on Christian believers until the courage of a girl, called Natasha, who he had beaten three times, affects him deeply. This leads to his own conversion. The book is now called Forgive Me, Natasha.

At high school we were all given a copy of the New English Bible. It was green with a hard cover. I wanted to read it but didn't want my parents to know. I used to keep it under my pillow and read bits in bed, hiding it away when Mum came in. Inside, I knew I was searching for something, something to complete me. I'd been told that we all have a 'God-shaped hole' inside us that only God himself can fully satisfy. I wanted that but wasn't ready yet.

George Banks became our new BB captain and, for five years, I went out with his middle daughter, Gillian. She was in the Girls Brigade. Our relationship was on and off but Gill's own faith, and that of her parents, would begin to influence me. George was quiet, calm and steady. I observed his patterns and routines in the home. He would always start and finish the day reading his Bible and praying. I could tell that he was building his life and family on good foundations.

At the church where we met, the Gladstone Mission, a man called Skip was in charge. He was a single man with a love for the local people that was reciprocated by their affection for him. He lived among them, married them, blessed their children, and buried their loved ones. He was particularly drawn towards the Romany and traveller families, who had settled in the neighbouring roads. They would all call the Mission their church, even though few attended, but they knew they could always pop to Skip's house for a cup of tea and a chat.

Dave and Pat had grown up under Skip's care and influence and used to run the young people's group after the Sunday evening service.

They would later take me under their wing and be instrumental in my nurture and coming to faith in Christ. Pat would become like a mum to my future wife, Jane.

I became a Christian when I was eighteen years old. It was at a tent crusade in Wallington. Dave and Pat took the youth group and when the invitation was given at the end of the meeting, I knew I was ready and that it was my time to fully surrender my life to God. Even as a teenager I knew the state of my own heart. I knew I needed forgiveness and that night I put my trust in Jesus Christ as my Saviour and Lord.

I did not understand everything then, but I knew that this was something I had to do. Some people claim to experience a Damascus Road conversion, with blinding lights and a voice from heaven, but mine was more akin to the Emmaus Road experience of walking with Jesus without recognising him. My heart was convicted and warmed as I realised that the God of Creation was calling me into his family, and that he had incredible plans and purposes for my new life.

From now on, I would learn to trust and follow the creator's instructions. I was ready for my new life's adventure!

KEVIN VICKERS

Chapter 7

Aramis and Arakis

"You'll calm down when you get older," someone said to me, but there and then I decided I wouldn't! I was going to be an all or nothing person for the rest of my life. I think I still am!

When I told my Mum that I'd become a Christian she got upset. Not because she was pleased but because she thought I was going to become all weird and religious. She thought she was going to lose her son. I have learnt that religion is our attempt to get to God and somehow get into his good books, but Christianity is the opposite. It is God's initiative to come and rescue us. We celebrate this at Christmas! I once sent a load of non-traditional Christmas cards that offended some people. The card had a smiley face and a sad face and read:

"This year, as usual, Santa Claus will bring all the kids who've been REALLY GOOD something nice for Christmas. The BEST present, however, is reserved for those who've been REALLY BAD. Funny isn't it?"

I'm not religious, but I know what people mean when they call me religious. I just want them to know that the other side of religion is the most personal and fulfilling relationship in the whole universe.

My favourite aftershave has always been Aramis. I'd put aside Hai Karate, Old Spice and Brut, and splashed out on the real stuff.

It was expensive even back then, but worth it. The smell would linger on for much longer than the cheaper brands.

I was once in the 'pound shop' in Mitcham where they were selling fragrances for men and women. There was one called Arakis. The packaging was similar but not the same as Aramis, but the smell was definitely the same! Wow! And for only one pound. I sprayed my hand, smelt it, amazing! I bought a few and left the shop. Outside I smelt my hand again – it was gone. The smell had gone! It was a fake, it was not the real thing.

I often tell that story when I am teaching on integrity because it holds an important lesson for me; a life lesson. I want to be the real thing and I want people who know and meet me to experience a genuine and authentic me. I try to be the same person wherever I am, and whoever I'm with. I hate pretence, hypocrisy and fake news. I can smell that a mile off. You probably can, too. Being real involves vulnerability and that can be costly. But it is worth the cost if we love people and want meaningful and healthy relationships.

I believe Jesus is the real thing, and I want to carry his fragrance in me and on me. I hope it will rub off on others.

GOBSMACKED

KEVIN VICKERS

GOBSMACKED

AT THE BANK

KEVIN VICKERS

Chapter 8

My First Proper Job

I did a paper round when I was thirteen and would race to be the first at the shop so that my papers were marked up before the others. I'd get there at 5:15am, just as the papers were being delivered from London, and before the shop was open.

The bakers' van would deliver bread to the shop and the driver would sometimes give me a free loaf of uncut bread, all nice and warm. I also did a butcher's round delivering meat before going to school. I rode a big black old-fashioned bicycle and sometimes fell off because my feet didn't reach the ground. On Saturday mornings, I'd work in the shop. One of my jobs was to clean the counters out the back but the smell of meat was so strong it made me sick. I asked my Mum to get me out of that job.

My first proper job after leaving school at sixteen was as a clerk at NatWest Bank at the Southfields branch. I had managed to get the job without the help of Mr Dunham, the careers adviser at school, who never seemed to do any work anyway. I'd visited the NatWest at the Whitgift Centre, Croydon, during half-term, and they'd willingly shown me around and gave me an application form. I got an interview in London and was offered a job pending my exam grades.

Apart from constantly resitting my English language exam, I never went to college or university. I started at the bank in a junior role and worked my way up. I loved it! I felt so proud and thought I had a job for life.

My first month's salary was £93.02 and I remember planning what I would do with all that money. I worked in the Machine Room, which means the back office where all the processing was done. I would learn to do the Rems, the Giros, the post, the statements and print the cheque books by hand. Printing cheque books was an occupational hazard back then and would never pass health and safety guidelines today. I am grateful to still have the five fingers on my left hand.

I was *Gobsmacked* at how fast Linda Therese could key the work on the B80 computer. All her fingers worked together at lightening speed. I got fast, too, but only with one finger and never as fast as Linda. My job was also to make the tea for everyone twice a day. I was glad to lose that responsibility when someone else joined and I was no longer the junior.

I wore a green three-piece suit from Burton's with brown shoes that had big heels. Why? I thought I was cool at the time! I progressed onto the tills and became a cashier. At 3.30pm each day we cashed up and agreed our tills. I loved it when I was right to the penny.

The Number One cashier was an older lady, and she was in charge. She knew most of the customers, particularly the businesses and pubs. We would buy money from her if we ran out and sell to her when we had surplus.

It was her job to always make sure we had enough cash on the premises and to balance the cash book at the end of the day. One day I would get to do that job, too.

In those days banking was not centralised, so each branch had a variety of jobs and responsibilities to learn. It was easy to see your next step and imagine a potential career path. I moved on to learn records, standing orders, and had a go at the SMO role, which stands for Senior Machine Operator. The person who did that job was in charge of the whole Machine Room. I wasn't very good at that and didn't like being in charge. I much preferred the jobs where I could work alone, take pride in what I did, pace myself, order my time and clear my desk at the end of each day. I didn't mind working late if it meant I could keep my work up straight.

I learned so much and was encouraged with lots of opportunities. I would take my turn 'manning' the enquiry counter, dealing with difficult customers, and handling the pressures and demands of increased responsibility. I was also socialising with my workmates at the NWB Sports and Social Club and learning how to navigate my newfound faith in the 'real world'.

After three full years at Southfields, I was transferred to Wimbledon Hill Road branch. I didn't know it then, but this would be where I would meet my wife over a game of chess.

KEVIN VICKERS

Chapter 9

Being Courted Over a Game of Chess

Wimbledon's branch was much bigger than Southfields and I immediately felt like a small fish in a big pond. Mr Pinney was the Manager, a pristinely dressed little man with an old-fashioned office from bygone days. He was like the Mr Pavitt of the banking world. He too had a wide grin.

Processes and practices are the same throughout the Bank, so it wasn't long before I was comfortable in my new setting and getting to know the staff. Mr Thompson was the Sub-Manager, a warm and approachable man who seemed to take a genuine interest in people's lives. He smoked a lot and seemed to suffer with his nerves. There were a lot of younger staff at the branch and always a buzz in the Machine Room.

Jane transferred from Hammersmith Broadway branch a little after I'd arrived. She had suffered bullying from her previous Sub-Manager, who seemed to have it in for her. She found Wimbledon a breath of fresh air and quickly fitted in. Jane was petite with blonde permed hair and a smiley face. She would wear different coloured berets with what I came to call her 'London Borough of Merton Workman's Coat'. Apparently, donkey jackets were fashionable at the time, but I never saw anybody else wearing one except when they were digging the roads.

She would move around the office at one hundred miles an hour; always on the go. They made Jane a key-holder because she was the first to arrive in the morning.

I first got to notice Jane when she was on the tills working as a cashier. I think I was working the foreign till at the time, and we would sometimes literally bump into one another. I now realise this was orchestrated by Jane who often just happened to be where I was.

The staff room was upstairs, and sometimes we would be on the same lunch hour. In a conversation one day, I must have mentioned that I could play chess. The following day Jane just happened to have with her a travel chess set and asked me for a game. I guess you could say she made the first move in our relationship!

One evening, we both happened to be leaving work at the same time. It was dark outside and as I opened the door Jane said, "Oh no I've just missed my bus, I think I'll go to McDonald's for a coffee". I found myself saying, "I'll come with you if you like?" And that was our first unofficial date.

This would be the first of two significant and defining moments in McDonald's; the second would take place some years later.

I was living at home with Mum and Dad before the time of mobile phones, when Jane rang the house phone and my mum answered it. She asked if I wanted to go for a walk along the River Thames at Hampton Court. I agreed and met her there. It was awkward to start with, but we got on well and seemed to have some really important things in common.

Jane knew that I was a Christian and asked me about my faith, church and youth group. I was now running the young people's group at church.

She told me that she attended Bible studies and I asked her more about these. As we walked side by side along the Thames, she reluctantly told me that they were Jehovah Witness Bible studies. I can remember walking the next few moments in silence because I didn't know what to say. She knew that this was a bombshell for our relationship which hadn't really got off the ground yet anyway. I wondered whether I should push her in the water and run. I decided against that!

We did talk more and Jane shared some of her story growing up at home after her dad had died when she was two years old. Her mum got involved with the JW's shortly after this, and Jane and her younger brother, Robin, were brought up to attend their meetings and follow their teachings. Her mum would remarry when Jane was in her early teens.

Jane would soon come to realise that by dating me she would be walking away from the Jehovah Witness community and suffer a huge cost in her own family.

So, this was the beginning of our courtship. Over the next few months, we would secretly meet for lunch at Coombs Bakery in Wimbledon where I would have pasty, chips, and beans. We would date at the Golden Tandoori Restaurant in Hartfield Road and Jane would start attending the young people's group at church. Our colleagues at work knew nothing of this until we arrived together at a work's darts match and Jane sat on my lap.

KEVIN VICKERS

Chapter 10

Night Safes and the Book Room Trolley

Every Monday morning, two people were rostered to count the money deposited over the weekend by shops and pubs. Cash and cheques were placed into little grey boxes, uniquely sealed with the customers ID, and dropped in the bank's night safe facility through a secure hole in the wall.

There were lots of them and sometimes it would take most of the day to count, agree and balance all the night safes. It was a boring and monotonous job, and on Mondays we would have to do it downstairs in the main safe room, where we were locked in for security and protection. I often got to do this with Noel O'Keefe, an older man with white hair, a melodic Irish accent and a wicked sense of humour. Noel was a lifelong cashier, and all the customers knew and loved him. Over time, Noel and I decided to make a meal of the night safes.

We started by sharing sandwiches, biscuits and cakes with tea and coffee. As weeks passed, it got more elaborate. One Monday morning, Noel brought in a red checkered tablecloth and a cask of white wine in a box. We wheeled in the book room trolley, covered it with the tablecloth and laid out our food and wine feast for the day. He'd also sneaked in two wine glasses! We'd eat, drink, listen to music and do the night safes.

Later, when Mr Thompson the Sub-Manager checked in on us, he nearly had a heart-attack. Over the weeks, he had come to accept that we were making the most of a laborious job and had largely overlooked our capers — but this time we had gone just a little bit too far. I can still see the utter shock and bewilderment on his face. He was truly *gobsmacked*, and at first did not know what to say. We knew that we'd overstepped the mark and that was probably the last time me and Noel did the night safes together!

The worst thing was when we couldn't agree and balance them at the end of the day. I wonder why? I remember Jane visiting us downstairs and the laughter the three of us would have together. Jane warmed to Noel, too, because he was such a loveable character and would tell funny stories, made even more interesting by his strong accent. He worked at his own slow pace, didn't rush, and was usually the last of the cashiers to till up when we closed.

One busy day, when he was serving a customer and with a long queue in the banking hall, I crept up behind him and lifted the lever on the side of his tall chair. The seat began to lower with Noel slowly disappearing below the eye line of the customer. I got a lot of fun out of doing crazy things like that.

Alan Timms was one of the Assistant Managers. He could be funny and nice and then change and be quite mean and unhelpful. Once the zip flies broke on my suit trousers and he would only spare me one small safety pin from his collection.

I dreaded writing letters to customers for him to sign because he would always change them, and I'd have to write them again. He could also be quite disrespectful to another Assistant Manager at the branch who was less able and a bit socially awkward. Other members of staff would pick up on this and join in.

I think I have a bias towards people who don't always fit in. I want to go after them, include them and show them that they are special, valued and significant. I want to make things right but know it's not always possible. I tried to do this at work with the other Assistant Manager. He was a lot older than me, but I tried to look out for him and champion him where I could. We had fishing in common, so that helped. We lost contact when I moved on, but I hope and pray that things worked out better for him in the future.

I stayed at Wimbledon branch for just over three years. I learnt the foreign till and by mistake, once sold Australian dollars at the exchange rate of Belgian francs. If only it was the other way around! I was gaining experience in a larger environment and given opportunities to train in tasks with more responsibility.

My night safe escapade with Noel was not held against me, and Mr Thompson still smiled from time to time.

KEVIN VICKERS

Chapter 11

When Promotion is slow coming

After an annual review, I was recruited to do training and relief work for the bank across the South West London area. I needed to be very flexible and prepared to travel to different branches as the need arose week on week. Sometimes, I'd be training people on the job and at other times I'd be covering a role due to staff sickness or holiday.

I was now competent in most of the clerical roles and enjoyed my new responsibilities immensely. Although it was often challenging and demanding, I was up for it and learnt to handle and thrive under pressure, meet deadlines, and manage heavy workloads. I enjoyed some branches more than others and made some my favourites. I used to like going to Cobham branch, where I worked on the commercial foreign desk. Ewell branch was very quiet. The cashiers would start balancing their tills the moment the doors shut, and we would all be out and going home by 4pm! My least favourite was Richmond. It was difficult to get to, crazily busy and there always seemed to be a backlog of work for me to catch up with. At one branch, which shall remain nameless, the Sub-Manager would spend every afternoon across the road in the snooker club, returning at 3.30pm to shut the doors. How did he get away with that?

Once, when I was covering the foreign till at a branch in Surrey, I received a call to say Cliff Richard would be calling to collect travel facilities the next day.

I have always been an opportunist, so I spoke to Dave at the Mission and persuaded him to write a letter for me to hand to Cliff inviting him to come and speak at our church for an outreach. Dave obliged and the next day when Cliff collected his travel money, I handed him my letter with a smile! He never came but we did get a nice reply from his agent. After this travelling season, I was appointed to a permanent role at Leatherhead branch. Here, I was trained in more senior positions and started to get my hopes up for promotion, but it would be a long time in coming.

I was at the top of the clerical grades and looking for my first appointment to management. They moved me to Stockwell branch, where I was the Manager's Clerk and asked to deputise for the Assistant Manager, as well as cover at the sub-branch in Kennington down the road. When Kennington branch closed, I salvaged a nearly new L-shaped workstation, and it has been my desk at home ever since. After Stockwell, I was transferred to Tooting branch.

Tooting was a big branch with a Senior Manager, Lending Manager, Sub-Manager and four Assistant Managers. I became one of the Manager's Clerks and it felt like I was going backwards in my career.

Alun Jones was the Senior Manager, a tall, proud Welshman whose life was banking. After a time, I became his clerk.

He expected much and I observed and learnt a lot from him. He used to say, "Turnover is vanity, profit is sanity." He once saw me walking back to the branch eating a portion of chips and chided me, "Kevin, is that good for the corporate image?" The answer was probably no, but I enjoyed the chips.

Once, we took a customer to lunch who was looking to review their borrowing. Later that afternoon, Mr Jones told me that he would expect my full report on his desk first thing in the morning. It was my birthday that day, so I told him that I thought he was being totally unreasonable because I had made plans for that evening. Surprisingly, after that he mellowed towards me, and I saw another side of him. Later, I'd get to know him better, be able to tease him a bit, and we would meet up after he retired.

Others around me were moving on, but I could not see my way forward. I felt jealous of others' success. I was not in a good place. Then, one day, as I was walking home from work over Colliers Wood Bridge, I looked up at the sky and felt a peace and contentment come over me. It was then that I prayed a prayer and meant every word of it...

"Lord, I don't care if I remain a grade five clerk for the rest of my life, as long as I stay in your will and purpose, I will trust you".

Within a few weeks of that prayer, I was promoted to an Assistant Manager. I don't know how it works, but I do know that my faith grew through that experience, and I learned to depend on God for my future.

KEVIN VICKERS

Chapter 12

Another Defining Moment at McDonald's

My favourite role as an Assistant Manager was in lending. I had my own office next door to the two managers, a clerk, who would support me, and manage my diary, and my own portfolio of customers. I would conduct lending interviews throughout the day.

Mr Jones would often put his head around the door and pop in for a chat. I always felt I could run the more complex cases by him and be guided by his vast knowledge and lifelong experience. He was a stern looking man, but I managed to get past that front and make him laugh. He knew I was a Christian and sometimes would scribble wise sayings or proverbs on the bottom of my paperwork. I would send him little messages, too. I think he secretly liked me.

In those days, we all had discretionary powers to lend money up to a certain limit. I could lend up to £5,000 unsecured and £30,000 secured. I was trained to know what to look for, and every proposition was judged on its own merits. Sometimes, it would come down to a gut feeling! Today, these decisions are largely made by computers using an elaborate credit scoring process.

The bank launched a new initiative called Project Harvest, and I was asked to be part of it. It was a pilot programme for two years aimed at attracting new start-up businesses.

Each business would benefit from having its own Relationship Manager, called a Small Business Adviser, and I would be trained along with a dozen others across the country to run the pilot. We all got given a briefcase, a name badge, a hospitality budget, and a lot of freedom. I still have the briefcase! Although I was based at Tooting, I enjoyed a more autonomous role. I was largely my own boss and would work on my initiative to generate new business for the bank. I loved it!

I made friends with Mr Tariq, a businessman on the high street, and would often pop into his shop for mid-morning samosas with him and his wife I would walk my patch around the markets and get to know the stall holders. I learnt this from Mr Jones, who used to practice what is called MBWA, meaning 'Managing By Wandering Around'.

I offered to do a talk on bank charges at the Asian Traders Association and threw myself to the lions that day, but came out with more credibility than I went in with, by addressing the elephant in the room. Once, I had to do a presentation on my new role, so I decided to use visual aids. I had three very young children, so I chose some of their toys to help me. I used water wings, a telephone on wheels, and a plastic stethoscope. I spoke about the need for new start-up businesses to keep afloat. How they would benefit from a personal relationship manager at the end of a phone, and an annual health check. What I did then with those three visual aids would influence how I would teach in the future. Visual aids would always be part of my life!

At church, I was running the Young People's Fellowship and given regular opportunities to lead services and sometimes even preach the sermon. I took it very seriously then and still do now. I wanted to study the Bible more, to train and to learn how to lead well. Dave was the Bible teacher at church and would produce comprehensive notes that I would read and keep. He encouraged my studies and invested much in me. I was also made the church treasurer – for obvious reasons! At the age of thirty, I was invited to become an elder and serve on the leadership. I was the younger elder!

'Project Harvest' was nearing completion and I was feeling more and more compelled to go to Bible college and study for a full-time role as a Pastor. It would mean leaving the bank and the financial security that it offered. This was a massive test of faith for me and Jane.

Jane was now a stay-at-home mum, and our children were five, four and two years old. It seemed foolish, but after prayer, and time, we were prepared to trust God and step out. Thirty minutes before my exit interview with Susan Law, the Deputy Regional Director, I sat in McDonald's at Croydon. It was 2.30pm on the 2nd March, 1993 when I wrote my prayer on A4 lined paper. I told God what I was about to do and why I was doing it. I wrote statements from the Bible that we were trusting in from Proverbs 3:5-10. I crossed all the t's and dotted all the i's. I made sure that God clearly understood the enormity of what I was about to do and asked him to stop me if it was wrong.

I folded the paper, put it in my pocket and left McDonald's. Excited, but also scared, I crossed the road for my 3pm appointment where I planned to hand in my resignation.

KEVIN VICKERS

Chapter 13

The Best of Both Worlds

I had not met Susan Law before, but she was gracious and attentive and listened to my nervous speech. She asked me a lot about what I wanted to do in the future and how my plans were progressing. I told her that I wanted to attend Spurgeon's Bible College from October to train in biblical theology and Old and New Testament studies. I also wanted to be available to work for the church in a pastoral role while I was training. I didn't have all the details confirmed or sorted yet.

She told me that the bank was exploring more flexible working patterns for male members of staff like me in management positions. She sowed the idea of working part-time for the bank whilst at the same time training for the Christian ministry. This possibility had never occurred to me. Although I was trying to hand in my notice, Susan suggested that we keep this meeting off the record and meet again in a month's time. She wanted me to go away and confirm my plans to study and she would go away and consider other possible options for keeping me employed with NatWest Bank.

Walking to the train station, I knew that my prayers were being answered. My future was being guided by my Heavenly Father; He had gone before me. A month later, I returned for the follow-up meeting with Susan Law.

I had finalised my theological training for Monday evenings at Bible college over three years, and I would serve my church in a voluntary pastoral role during the day.

Susan offered me a career change redundancy package to go part-time two-and-a-half days a week under a new scheme the bank was launching. I accepted! I would retain my grade as an Assistant Manager and went on to be featured in a book of case studies promoting flexible working and equal opportunities. I also got my photo in a national newspaper. The timing was perfect for me and I would now enjoy the best of both worlds.

I would work as the Assistant Manager of Clapham Common branch on their busiest days – Mondays and Fridays – from 1993 to 1996. The bank had further agreed to reduce my hours to two full days, allowing me the other three to pursue my pastoral work.

I once interviewed a couple who wanted a loan for their wedding and I had to decline the loan, unfortunately, but I did offer to marry them. I never actually did, but they left the meeting in good spirits. I was honoured to be asked to do a marriage blessing for a colleague at work, and support another through difficult times. After three years I was seconded by the bank to Croydon Business Venture, an enterprise agency offering help and advice to start-up businesses. I would run the Introduction to Running Your Own Business half-day seminar every Monday morning and the rest of my time was spent in interviews supporting start-ups. Some of those start-up businesses were also renting office space onsite. I had my own office alongside my full-time, and more experienced colleagues, Mel and John.

I saw my work at the bank, the enterprise agency, and the church as overlapping, and I'd aim to give my best in all I did.

One complimented the other and kept my feet on the ground and my faith relevant to the stresses and strains of everyday life.

I would sometimes get the opportunity to share the other side of what I did with clients who were interested. Sometimes, I'd offer to pray for them. I'd be careful not to preach or use religious jargon and keep within the professional boundaries expected of me. Also, I once took a funeral in my lunch hour!

One Monday, I was in my office after a long and tiring day. The man renting the office next door would often pop in for a chat, and he could talk a lot. I was tired and struggled to keep my eyes open as I laid back in my comfortable swivel chair. The next thing I knew he was waking me up because I'd dozed off to sleep. Totally embarrassed, I couldn't stop apologising. The same thing happened when I was sharing a room with a friend on a trip to Israel. We took it in turns to say a prayer at the end of the day before we went to sleep. Ben, never short of words, prayed one night and went on and on and I fell asleep. He had to wake me up too! We laughed about it, I apologised, but when it was his turn to pray again the same thing happened and I fell asleep!

I loved my three years at Croydon Business Venture and miss my weekly visits to Cherry Orchard Café, where I would enjoy two sausages, egg and chips, two slices of toast without butter and a mug of coffee with half a sugar. They would prepare my order without me asking.

As I sat in my office on Friday, the 22nd October, 1999, I knew it was time to complete my transition from banking to full-time church work. My NatWest boss was due to arrive at 11am. I had 35 minutes to write out my next prayer.

Chapter 14
Let NOTHING Be Wasted

When my NatWest secondment finished in January 2000, I would finally say my goodbyes to the bank. Under their 'New Directions Package', I was offered a full and final redundancy lump sum, even though I'd once again tendered my resignation to pursue full-time work as a Pastor. I saw God's timing and hand in this and felt nothing but gratitude for my twenty-two years as a NatWest Bank employee.

On the 7th December, 1999, following my formal interview with my boss, I wrote to Susan Law thanking her for the significant part she had played in my journey. She had expressed concern for our family finances, and I wanted to tell her that God had been faithful in providing for us, and that he had used her to help make it happen. I don't know if she ever received my letter, but if she did; I hope it blessed her heart and moved her closer to trust God, too.

When Jesus fed the five thousand with the boy's packed lunch, he told his disciples to go and pick up the leftovers. "Let nothing be wasted," he said. They filled twelve baskets with the pieces left over. I love this story, but the lesson for me here is that nothing in my life's journey need ever be wasted or lost. I want to carry forward what I have learnt and experienced and use it to be stronger and wiser myself and help nourish others. Even the bad, the hard, and the worst times can be redeemed and turned into good.

I plan to be a life-long learner, always better, and never bitter.

Now as a church leader I am still passionate about teaching others money management and offering budget coaching. Our church recently ran a 'Debt Centre' for the community. I get asked by business managers in primary schools to audit their school fund accounts because of my banking background, and I love to sit with small business owners and discuss business plans, cashflow forecasts and marketing initiatives.

I've also taken a leaf out of Mr Jones's book and regularly practice 'Managing By Wandering Around' when I walk my patch, pray for my community, and engage with the real issues affecting people lives.

GOBSMACKED

KEVIN VICKERS

It's not Terry's, It's mine.

GOBSMACKED

IN MY FAMILY

KEVIN VICKERS

Chapter 15

Jane and the Importance of Christmas

Jane and I were married on the 7th June, 1986 by Skip at the Gladstone Mission in Mitcham. Yellow is one of Jane's favourite colours because it is bright and cheerful, and this was reflected in the flowers, decorations, and the bow ties that Mike and I wore. Jane's Nan came, and her favourite uncle, Dave, gave her away. Her niece, Nicola, was our one and only bridesmaid, also in yellow, and Jane's other two uncles and aunts celebrated the day with us.

The reception hall was decorated elaborately with yellow and white paper chains, which one of the children pointed out looked like toilet paper – they were right, it was! In the evening we had a barn dance. We changed clothes at Dave and Pat's house a few doors from the Mission, where I dressed as a cowboy and Jane wore a gingham dress as a cowgirl. It was a perfect day tinged only by the absence of Jane's mum, stepdad and brother.

When we started dating, Jane was given an ultimatum by her mum to either break up with me or move out. She had stopped going to the JW meetings and had started to question their beliefs. After a visit from their elders, Jane was disfellowshipped from the organisation and requested to break ties with family and JW friends.

She moved out of the family home and rented a room in Kingston Hill. Later, she would find an attic room in Merton Park during the week and stay at my mum and dad's at weekends.

I was not fully aware of what Jane was going through or the cost she was paying for her decision to be with me. I did discover, though, that she lived off risotto for days on end.

Jane is a private person and rarely shows her feelings. She's an overcomer and just gets on with things. Her courage and fortitude have been remarkable. Instead of rejecting her mum and brother, or holding a long-term grudge, she continued to reach out to them. She found it in her heart to leave the hurt and pain with God, and to forgive, grace and pursue her family. It tends to be one-way, but we believe that that is how love wins in the end. Over time, we have been able to visit her mum, who is now remarried, and things have been easier as time has passed. We keep in touch with Jane's bother, Robin, and his wife, Kay, more often.

Jane became a Christian at a Luis Palau evangelistic event on 14th October, 1983. I was not there but this would be a significant turning point in her life and in cementing our future relationship. Our hearts were joined in our faith in Christ, and we would marry just under three years later.

JW's do not celebrate birthdays or Christmas, so Jane had some catching up to do. We must have a real Christmas tree, the biggest one we can get into the front room, and Jane is the only one allowed to decorate it.

Even when our children were at home, they knew that the Christmas tree was mum's job, and hers alone! She can be very possessive when it comes to presents, too. Like a child beginning to get excited about Christmas Day for the first time, Jane is the first up, sitting on the floor, and dividing the presents into piles so that we can start opening them as soon as possible!

Her 'love language' is gifts. They haven't got to be expensive, but woe betide anyone who wants a piece of her Terry's Chocolate Orange. She will say, "It's not Terry's, it's **MINE**. Get your thieving hands off it!" Every year, I do Jane a Christmas stocking and put it at the bottom of her bed when I think she's asleep on Christmas Eve. As well as the chocolate orange, she'll get some liquorice, a box of matchmakers, a tangerine, and a walnut. She doesn't even like tangerines!

We currently have three grandchildren, and Jane makes it her priority to see them all every week if she can. She started working a four-day week after our first grandson, Nathan, was born so she could be around to spend time with him. Growing up, our children did not know a nan in their lives from Jane's side of the family, but that will not be the case now for theirs.

One of Jane's favourite verses in the Bible spoken by Jesus is this:

> *"No one who has left home or brothers or sisters or mother or father or children ... for me and the gospel will fail to receive a hundred times as much in this present age ... and in the age to come, eternal life."*
>
> **Mark 10:29-30 (NIV)**

I know Jane is grateful for the abundance of fathers and mothers, brothers, and sisters that God continues to bless her life with! Our children have their own homes and families now. And, at last, get to decorate their own Christmas trees.

Chapter 16

When the Neighbours Call the Police

Mike and I were both born in the front bedroom of 7 Hawthorne Avenue five years apart. In fact, Mike reminds me that he did everything five years after me! He became a Christian, got baptised, had an unsuccessful interview with the bank, and got married – all five years after me.

We moved to 38 Hawthorne when I was nineteen years old, and my Mum still lives there now. Apart from a 14-month stay five minutes away in SW19 after we were married, I have always lived in Mitcham. We moved to our present home in Oakwood Avenue in August 1987, two months before our first son, Samuel, was born. From my little office window, I can still see the back upstairs window of the house where I grew up, where Addy put the hose on the 'Effing-Graves', all those years ago.

Samuel David was born on the 1st October at 12.09pm, weighing 5lb 14½oz. There was a student midwife assisting and he was one side of Jane whilst I was at the other helping her to push. I was exhausted at the end and felt like I'd given birth! Jane was helped by the gas and air, which made her giggle a bit in between contractions but the pethidine took too long to kick in. It was also a scary moment when the baby was born with the umbilical cord around his neck. All three of ours were born the same. What were they doing?

We chose the name Samuel because it means 'God has heard', and in the Bible, young Samuel gets to hear the voice of God speaking to him. This has always been our prayer and hope for our son Samuel.

We were first-time parents and didn't want to get it wrong. He was so small. We'd keep checking on him when he was asleep in his cot to make sure he was breathing. We would have his pram beside our bed and for those first few months, Jane would rock the pram with one hand whilst she laid in bed half asleep, half awake. One evening, a few months later, we were both exhausted because the baby was constantly crying. He'd been fed, changed, picked up, put down, rocked...but nothing seemed to help. That evening we just couldn't get him to settle.

We had both raised our voices, "Go to sleep!" We were overtired, stressed, and not knowing what to do. Eventually, Samuel went to sleep. Jane carefully carried him upstairs to the middle bedroom where she placed him in his new cot. She closed the door and crept downstairs – peace at last!

It wasn't long after this that there was a knock on the front door. I answered it. Two policemen were standing there, I hesitated with complete shock. I then realised that a neighbour must have called the police because of the shouting they'd heard. They were polite and came in and one of them asked to see the baby. Jane pleaded with him not to wake Samuel. We took him upstairs where he went into the bedroom, checked everything was okay and then they graciously left us. As they went, I peered down the road to see if the neighbours were watching.

We felt like the worst parents in the world; totally ashamed and worried that others would find out and talk about us. What would they say at church if they knew? "How could I be a leader of God's people if I couldn't even manage my own family?"

It took us a long time to honestly talk about this to others. But, when we did, we found compassion rather than condemnation. We realised that in sharing and being vulnerable others could also share and identify with us. Instead of destroying my work serving others, it seemed to bring me closer to those I wanted to help. And it still does.

The following day we phoned the doctor, who was on call, and he told us to bring Samuel to his house in Merton Park because he could tell we were so worried. It was a lovely house and he was a kind doctor. He told us that Samuel had colic and gave us a prescription for something that would help. He also reassured us that we were doing our best.

I still drive past that house and remember the kindness of the doctor.

KEVIN VICKERS

Chapter 17
Creating Memories

Rob Parsons is one of my hero writers. He runs an organisation called Care for the Family, and over the years has written lots of books in a series called 'The 60 Minute...Father, Mother, Marriage, Grandparent'.

They are designed to be read in about an hour and are jammed-packed with heart-warming practical ideas. The books are written to create precious lifelong memories in any family. He is a Christian writer, but his books are not full of religious sentiment; instead they burst with wisdom and insights common and relevant to all. I want to write like him! I don't know Rob personally, but his books have been such a great help to me and my family.

Rachel Elizabeth was born on 1st December, 1988 at 1.05pm, weighing 6lb 5½oz. Her name means 'female sheep'. We laugh at the biblical significance of her name, but truly Rachel has a pastoral heart, and she loves people. We would see this later when she worked among the single mums and orphans in Dunoon, a township in Cape Town, South Africa, serving for three years with the most vulnerable and in the most dangerous of environments.

Jonathan Andrew is our youngest and was born two years later, on 14th December, 1990 at 12:32am, weighing 6lb 4oz. Jonathan means 'gift from God' and his coming would complete our young family.

Life in the Vickers' household would never be quiet or dull but always full of fun and craziness.

Box Hill has always been a favourite place of ours. We would sometimes park at the bottom in the car park, where the bikers gather to show off and admire their motorbikes, and we'd climb the grass verge to the top of the hill. We knew we were nearly there when we saw the Headstone of Peter Labelliere, an eccentric resident of Dorking, who was buried on the hill head downwards, on 11th June, 1800. A little bit further and we would be at the viewing point with its stunning panoramic views across the Surrey Hills.

Sam, Rach and Jon were highly competitive, and Rachel would not be outdone by her brothers. In the forest, we would make dens, and bury a note or sock or something in a plastic bottle and hope to find it next time we came. We would finish our trip by climbing down the steepest side on our bottoms. This was, and still is, dangerous, but a lot of fun.

The first time I took Jonathan, he was about five. It had been raining so it was very muddy and Jon slipped and tumbled down and out of sight. My heart was in my mouth as the rest of us slid after him. When we caught up, miraculously, he was OK. Shaken and scratched by brambles, but OK! We'd cross the River Mole at the bottom by way of the stepping-stones, and back at the car, the children had to take off all their dirty clothes before they could get in. We often travelled home with the three of them half-naked in the back seat! It got more interesting the older they got.

Another time, I took the three of them to Box Hill in the freezing cold winter for a picnic. We did something similar in Richmond Park once!

All of them learnt how to throw a frisbee. We would see how many times we could throw it to one another and catch it without dropping it. Then we would have to beat the record. We'd do the same with a bat and ball...we still do. We would never walk to the park, we'd always run; sometimes jumping over the cracks in the paving stones or walking to the first tree/lamp post and then running to the next, and so on.

I tried to spend individual time with each of them as they were growing up but I didn't always get this right. Once, Rachel told me she'd read in the church newsletter that I was going on a trip. Ah, I had told others before my children, not something I wanted to do again. They all loved football. The boys played Little League in Mitcham and Rachel was in a girl's league in Morden. I would often take Rachel and be asked to run a line which I hated. I didn't fully understand the offside rule and some parents took it so seriously that I sometimes got shouted at for my decisions or lack of them. I sometimes missed Jon's games because I was at Rachel's.

We had some amazing holidays at La Ranolien campsite and holiday park in Brittany, France, when the children were at their first school. We would go in June because it was cheaper, and we got permission to take them out of school. The car would be packed to the hilt with everything but the kitchen sink, including a roof box on top with bikes on the back.

We'd pick the three of them up just before school finished and they would sit on their sleeping bags covering the back seat of the car. Each had a plastic zipped folder with colouring book, pencils, quizzes, games and sweets. This was to keep them quiet while we travelled to the car ferry port at Portsmouth, but it never worked!

Sam, Rach and Jon still sing the 'Tiger Club' songs from those holidays. Jonathan remembers them the best. Sam recently prepared a zipped plastic holiday folder for his son, Nathan, with a colouring book, pencils, quizzes, games and sweets!

Chapter 18
The 'Vickers Gene'

Humour plays a major part in our family culture. We try not to take ourselves too seriously and laugh a lot when we're together. Mike and I both have long suffering wives and when our families meet up, it's always a lot of fun. Our favourite comedians are Harry Hill and Tim Vine, both as crazy as each other.

I live by the proverb that says:

> *"A cheerful heart is good medicine."* One of my special Bible verses is, *"..the joy of the LORD is your strength."*
>
> **Proverbs 17:22 (NIV)**

When we were younger and out shopping with Mum, Mike and I would find it funny to hang items of clothing – usually from the lingerie section – on the back of Mum's coat. She would walk around the shop without realising it. We'd also put small things in her hood and get her to try on all the different hats. When we went out for a meal, we'd sneak the salt and pepper and knives and forks into her handbag or coat pockets. My children do the same whoever they're with, and our seven-year-old grandson, Nathan, recently hid his auntie's coat and car keys when we were all together.

My children learnt that the car doors didn't open unless we all jumped up in the air at the same time. That worked for a while with the kids, but Jane refused to jump and threatened to kick the car if I didn't open the doors. Shopping in Sainsbury's can be fun when you meet a church member and secretly slip extra items into their trolley when they're not looking! Years ago, we had lots of different shaped glass bottles on our mantelpiece, and I named them after people in the church.

The children were a nightmare for babysitters and most only came once! Our three children would meticulously plan and make tricks and traps for them. From the trip wire at the top of the stairs, the books gingerly balanced on the partially open bedroomed door, to the Airfix aeroplane attached by string to the light fitting in the middle of the room, triggered to fly as the door swung open. Poor Ann Sherman! They would promise to go to sleep if the babysitter would read the book of their choice from cover to cover – usually the longest book they could find.

Every year, we would host students from Kingdom Faith Bible College as interns on work experience. I was the Pastor of the church and would plan their weekly schedules. Once, without me knowing, my children told the three new interns that dad had organised a 5:30am prayer meeting at the church that they needed to attend. Of course, when they got there the church was locked. On another occasion, one of the interns, called Steve, offered to give the children a lift home from church. They directed him all around the houses for about an hour and made him swear.

My children have a tendency of following my example and sometimes going too far, and, as Jane says, not knowing when to stop!

We didn't have a lot of money back then, but found that God provided for us in special ways. The church family would care for us. Envelopes of cash would be posted through our letterbox anonymously. I had budgeted the redundancy monies from the bank and was amazed at how far it went. If I was asked to officiate at a funeral service and received payment for it, the children would inappropriately cheer at the prospect of us having a takeaway later that evening. Before the days of Happy Meals, a family trip to McDonald's would involve me buying individual burgers and the largest Coke. I'd also ask for four small cups so I could divide the soft drink between the five of us. The children would have to wait until they were sixteen before they could have a set meal!

We are all very competitive, especially Jane. We all like to win, but can also be good losers – except Jane! Our friends know never to play Monopoly with the Vickers family because we cheat; not in a bad way but in a fun way, by hiding the money or stealing the property cards or winding other people up! Sue Pickett from church will never play with us again and needed counselling afterwards. Nathan loves to play Monopoly with us, too, and we have been teaching him that it's okay when you don't win.

I have learnt that a cheerful heart and an inward joy are not dependant on my circumstances but on a peace inside that only comes from God. That was about to be put to the test...

KEVIN VICKERS

Chapter 19

Jon's Accident in the USA (1)

When the house phone rings at 4.15am it's probably not good news. It wasn't! I answered the call from a lady in the USA who told me she was the aunt of Whitney, Jonathan's American girlfriend. Jon was serving his second summer as a children's camp counsellor with Voyageurs Lutheran Ministry in Cook, Minnesota. She told me there had been an accident and Jon had been involved in a serious car crash. She had no more details except to tell us to contact the hospital where he had been taken in Duluth.

Jane was with me now, downstairs, and I tried to relay the message to her as I was processing it. I anxiously got through to the hospital and spoke to a nurse in the Neuro Trauma Intensive Care Unit. Jon was alive; but he was in a critical condition on a life support machine. We were urged to go as soon as possible.

None of us had ever been to America before but we knew we were going now. Samuel was living in London with his partner Jo. Rachel was at home with us. We gathered, we prayed, we trusted God and we contacted people. Family, church family, friends from school and work. Everyone wanted to help us get there. After throwing some bits into a small case and collecting our passports, Dick and Ann drove me, Jane and Rach to Gatwick airport.

Sam would meet us there. As we travelled, staff friends at the Cricket Green School – where Jane, Rachel and Jon work, our church meets, and where I am governor – researched our required documentation and helped direct us to the right terminal and airline.

At Gatwick, we met up with Sam and after explaining the urgency of our travel at the airline desk, within two hours we were on a flight to Minnesota with a short layover in Chicago. Whitney's sister and her husband picked us up from the airport and drove us the three hours to St Mary's hospital in Duluth. Jane was travel sick for the duration of the drive. It was 3rd July, 2013, and it felt like the longest day ever. We had started the day at 4.15am in England, and it was now after 11pm in the US. We had arrived at the hospital the same day and made our way to intensive care.

Jon was unconscious when we saw him. There were tubes everywhere, and his head was heavily bandaged. We met the nurse I had spoken to on the phone that morning; and he was kind and surprised to see us so quick. We were told that Jon had sustained brain damage and several fractures in the accident. It was early days. Rachel stayed the first night with Jon while the rest of us tried to rest and sleep in the Sheraton Hotel on the hospital complex. We decided that we would take it in turns staying with him overnight, although I wouldn't cope with this very well.

The next day was 4th July, American Independence Day. I decided that all our dependence would be on God for Jon's full recovery. We would pray and ask others to pray too, all over the world.

We set up a Facebook page as our primary means of communicating with friends and family, called 'Jon Vickers Support Group', and Rach and myself would keep this site regularly updated.

Jon and four other camp counsellors were on a break and heading home to celebrate 4th July when the accident happened. Apparently, they missed a stop sign at an intersection and collided with a tractor trailer. The car was pinned beneath the trailer, which was hauling wheat, and the car caught fire. Libby, aged nineteen, was in the back seat and died on impact. Jon was asleep in the front seat when it happened and was trapped in the car after the others were got out. Local volunteer firefighters and ambulance staff managed to get to the scene quickly because they were all together nearby at their monthly training session. The car was crushed beneath the trailer with Jon still in it until a quick-thinking employee of the county public works, who also happened to be one of the volunteer ambulance drivers at the scene, drove about a mile to retrieve a John Deere front-end loader to lift the trailer, allowing the emergency services to tow out the car and free Jon. I've discovered the man's name was Dave Rankilla, who the day after would hand in the key to the county garage and retire on his sixty-second birthday after twenty-eight years of service.

Dave and the other members of the volunteer emergency services were later honoured with a 911 Lifesaver Award by the St Louis County Sheriff for their selfless bravery on that day.

On the 5th July three of their team turned up at the hospital to see how everyone was doing...

KEVIN VICKERS

Chapter 20
Jon's Accident in the USA (2)

The hospital covered our accommodation costs at the Sheraton Hotel for a week and we spent most of that time at Jon's bedside. The response from people was overwhelming. Our first Facebook update on the 4th July read:

> *"We can tell Jon is fighting, in the last 2 hours they've taken the draining tube out of his head and he's off the ventilator. We're hearing what a miracle his progress has been in the last day and a half. I've just come out of a meeting with the Camp Director (Joel), who arrived at the hospital when Jon first got here. He was honest in saying he prayed with the Chaplain, and they didn't think Jon was going to make it. A long way to go, but praising God for the journey to victory!"*

Messages, prayers and gifts were streaming in from friends all over the place. We were being sustained with an incredible peace inside as we celebrated Jon's progress moment by moment. Jon's other three friends in the accident were recovering well and being discharged. Whitney's mum and dad also supported us at the hospital and kept us stocked up with homemade chocolate brownies. Cricket Green School sent us messages and recorded Bob Marley's song in assembly: "Don't worry about a thing, cause every little thing gonna be alright".

Back home, I'd been teaching a series called, Everyday Faith. Now, we were practising what I was preaching. The prayer life of our church increased dramatically, and some people whose faith had lapsed found it reignited. Hospital staff told us they were praying, and the Lutheran Church in the State of Minnesota and beyond were called to prayer.

One afternoon, we left Jane with Jon, while Rach, Sam and me went to a nearby restaurant for a lunchtime snack. In the queue for food, a lady overheard our British accent and cheerily asked us if we were on holiday in Duluth. I explained that we were at the hospital because our son had been in an accident, to which she cried, "Jon Vickers?" When I said "yes" she started to cry and insisted on buying our food. She said her church had been praying and that she was in Duluth with her husband for the Bob Dylan concert. Later, they would come to the hospital with free tickets for Rach and Sam.

Catherine Anderson, who was associated with the Camp Ministry, let us live in her house for two weeks while she went on holiday to Switzerland. Rach and I would cycle to the hospital along Lake Superior and Jane and Sam would catch the bus for the fifteen-minute journey into town every day. We met Bishop Tom and his wife Becky, who invited us over for a meal. He was a beer-making bishop and Sam took to him straight away. He was interviewed about the accident and said in a newspaper report, "God was not in the accident, but in the healing." I liked Tom a lot!

Once, Tom stopped his car and handed me an envelope with money in it that had been collected by the Lutheran Church. People were so kind. We were taken out for meals, given a gift card to buy clothes from Target, entertained at people's homes and on lakes, and had access to as much ice cream as we could eat from Coldstone Creamery. All we had to do was go to the shop and say the magic words, "Jon Vickers", and we could order whatever we wanted for free. I tried this at the barber's shop because I needed a haircut. I told the barber all about Jon's accident and when he'd finished cutting my hair, he said twenty dollars please. Jon's name never worked at the barbers!

Jon continued to make progress and after five days he was stepped down from intensive care to intermediate care. Joel would say, "Jon quite literally seems to improve by the hour."

On the 9th July, a memorial service was held at Camp Vermilion for Libby, overlooking the lake, where her ashes would be scattered. Jane stayed with Jon but the rest of us attended with Libby's mum, dad and two older brothers. I remember hugging her mum and feeling guilty that my son was still alive whilst her daughter had died. She said to me they were all okay because they knew where Libby was. I realised that God was sustaining them with a grace that I did not have because I didn't need it. He was gracing us with faith to believe for Jon's full healing. The night before they had visited us at the hospital and embraced Whitney who had been driving the car at the time of the accident. The next day Jon graduated to the general trauma ward.

I struggled to stay with Jon overnight as he would pull at the wires and tubes attached to him and try to take off his neck brace. Jane and Rachel were much better at coping with this than me. Jon's friend, Cory, a canoe guide at camp visited with her guitar and sang some camp and worship songs. It blessed our heart to watch Jon joining in with some of the words.

On the 11th July, they moved Jon across the skywalk to rehab. A team of therapists planned his road to recovery. They worked on him for four hours a day and by the end of it he was exhausted. They did lots of mind and logic games to retrain his brain to make new pathways where it had been damaged. He had double vision for a while and wore an eyepatch like a pirate! On the 14th July, we were able to post the first picture of Jon lying on his bed attempting a smile with his thumbs raised. We knew people were waiting for this and the response was incredible. The day after we had a surprise visitor. Our church was doing a weekly video Bible study called Crucible, taught by Phil Tuttle, the President of 'Walk Thru the Bible Ministries' in Atlanta, USA. Hayley, one of our members, emailed Phil and told him that we were facing our own crucible right now. Phil flew from Atlanta to be with us at the hospital and pray with Jon.

Jon was miraculously recovering and every day we saw some improvement. Joel, the camp director organised and encouraged some light relief for us during this time. Rachel and I visited the Mall of America in Minnesota. We went jet skiing on one of the lakes and I got to fly a four-man aeroplane over the camp. Jon's discharge date was the 6th August, but he was determined to get out sooner.

He was discharged earlier on the 2nd August, exactly one month after the accident had happened, with a referral to continue treatment when we returned to the UK. By now we were living in the basement with the Grunwalds – the parents of one of Jon's counsellor friends, and Sam had returned home to go back to work.

We finished our stay in America at Camp Hiawatha, because Jon insisted on attending the annual bluegrass festival marking the end of the summer camps. Two days later, on the 12th August, we all flew home for a family reunion at Heathrow airport.

Jon is now a qualified special needs teacher at Cricket Green School. He teases us frequently about our 'holiday' in America. As if!

KEVIN VICKERS

Chapter 21

You can't Have Nan and Toast in the Morning!

To some people, the Vickers humour may seem inappropriate at times, particularly when it relates to the way Mike and I treat my Mum. But we know she secretly enjoys it and, at eighty-four, it keeps her young!

My Mum's name is Shirley, and she has a friend called Shirley Few, who used to live down our road. My Mum always refers to her as Shirley Few, so we call her a 'few Shirley's'. Her husband, Alan, was an electrician and our 'go to' person if ever we had an electricity emergency. He was a kind man who drove a Reliant Robin and would tell us of his exploits working in Windsor Castle. We called him 'Electric Alan'.

After Dad died, Mum became good friends with another Alan, a Welshman, and a proper gentleman. Alan had one leg and would attend the luncheon club attached to the Mission. When Jane's mum remarried, she married Doug, who has one arm. We used to say they can't get a whole man between them! Alan asked my permission to propose to my Mum, but, sadly, it was not to be as Alan died shortly afterwards.

When Mike's family and mine get together with my Mum, it's always a bundle of laughs. We'll lift her up between us and carry her somewhere placing her down on a wall, table, skip or recycle bin.

Her regular saying when we tease her is, "Git out of it!"

For her eightieth birthday, we took her to a caravan site in Newport, on the Isle of Wight. She loves the island. We had two caravans between us and when we first arrived Rachel made a 'Sorry out of order' sign and put it on the toilet door in one of them. My Mum wanted to go, so we said she could use the other caravan. Rachel had put the same sign in the other caravan too. We were outside and suddenly heard her shout out, "I don't believe it." We were trying to hold it together when we were joined by a rep from the holiday site. Mum immediately started to complain to her about the state of the toilets and how bad it was that they were both broken. That was such a funny start to our short break away!

Mum always wanted to go to the Edinburgh Tattoo, so one year we took her. We were sitting high up in the stands as the performance was about to start when Mum stood up to take a picture with her Boots disposable camera. At the moment she pushed the button, a cannon went off with the loudest bang and we all jumped out of our skin laughing with the people behind at the thought that Mum's 'click' had set off the cannon to start the show.

Rachel was living at her nan's doing an online university design course. For one of her assignments, she had to outline on the floor the shape of a body with masking tape. She had my Mum lying on her bedroom floor looking like something out of CSI. The tape was left for so long that when it was taken up, it left a permanent mark of mum's body outline on the carpet, resembling a crime scene. She eventually replaced the carpet.

Recently, my Mum went to post a letter in the post box at the top of the road.

When she got there, she couldn't reach it without being on tiptoes. "Oh no." she thought, "I've shrunk." The Post Office had, apparently, raised the post box by about six inches to cater for an increase in letters, but my Mum thought she was getting smaller with age!

Harry Hill tells a story about visiting his nan in hospital who was on a life support machine. Apparently, there was a toaster nearby but only one plug. His punch line is: "You can't have nan and toast in the morning!"

Mike and his wife Sarah were celebrating twenty-five years of ministry in the church and friends of theirs were organising a special evening of worship, tributes, and fun. As part of this, we thought it would be funny to video Harry Hill's story using my Mum. She was game for it. Mike's friend, Alan, came to my Mum's house with his video camera and Mum went to bed. We put the toaster next to her with some toast in it and filmed mum sitting up smiling. Suddenly, the toast sprang up and Mum fell back on the pillar with a groan. We finished with the caption:

"You can't have nan and toast in the morning!"

When the clip was shown at Mike and Sarah's do, not everyone was roaring with laughter. Our family, including my Mum were, and those who knew us well. But some people probably considered our humour a tad inappropriate and a little too far!

KEVIN VICKERS

GOBSMACKED
AT CHURCH

KEVIN VICKERS

Chapter 22
My First Proper Church

The Mission was my first church. It was where I grew up at Boys Brigade, first became a Christian, was nurtured, encouraged, invested in and given responsibility. This was my first experience of a church family doing life together. We were not part of a large denomination but essentially an independent mission outpost of the Shaftesbury Society, commissioned to work and serve the local people. Over the years, Shaftesbury relinquished its mission work and sold off a lot of the premises – our church building was one of them.

I have always been drawn to pastoral work and see the value of investing in the lives of others, often just ones and twos. I am learning the difference between success and fruitfulness. Of course, I want to be successful, who doesn't? But I want that success to be lasting and not fleeting.

Success can usually be measured but it's harder to measure fruitfulness. Success can be seen; fruitfulness is often hidden. Fruit is something that gets enjoyed by others and can travel far and wide. The tree does not know where the fruit will end up and I want my life to be like that tree. I believe that God does more behind our backs than in front of our faces. Success is linked to competence whereas fruit is borne and grows through character.

The apostle Paul sums it up for me when he writes in one of his letters,

> *"I want to remain among you for your progress and joy in the faith."*

> **Philippians 1:25 (paraphrased)**

In other words, "I'm here for you."

I still have the notes of my first ever sermon. My text was, "If God is for us who can be against us?" I would write out every word and read it as written. I have just noticed that after the closing prayer I had written the word 'phew'. I am so grateful, now, that my leaders took a risk on me then.

I ran the Young People's Fellowship group for the twenties and thirty-year-olds and enjoyed close friendships with others around the same age. Some of us were getting married, having children and some moving away. I have great memories of mission weekends away at Whitstable and Herne Bay Court; Bank Holiday Rambles to Box Hill and Farthing Downs; annual pantomimes led by Pat Paine; and cleaning and maintenance week, where George and Crystal took the lead. Christmas was always very special and Ros would use her artistic gifts to decorate the big blue curtain at the front of the church. Pauline would organise a choir and the Christmas post box would be opened after the carol service, and we'd all get loads of cards. Skip would usually lead the sunrise service on Easter Day at 5.30am on Headley Heath.

We rarely saw the sun rise but always looked forward to a cooked breakfast back at church afterwards.

Mum started going to Ladies Night, run by Ann and Crystal, and would volunteer at the luncheon club. Auntie Brenda and Uncle Roy would attend the luncheon club, and Uncle Roy would go to Men's Night, run by Derek upstairs in the snooker room.

From the age of ten, the Mission was my second home for thirty-four years. My young life was planted in good ground. After leaving NatWest in the year 2000, I would be passionate about serving God's purposes in full-time ministry for the rest of my life. That passion, however, would not always show itself with wisdom and love. I'll come back to that later.

KEVIN VICKERS

Chapter 23

Funeral Stories

I was asked to take my first funeral and didn't know what to do, so I went to see Skip. Everyone went to see Skip when they didn't know what to do; he lived among the people, and they considered him one of their own. Skip had baptised me as a believer in Jesus Christ and took my Dad's funeral. He was wise, and always seemed to have the right words to say. He was godly and loved Jesus. I remember some of his sayings.

When someone would say, "Everyone's doing it," Skip would say, "Well, I'm NOT!"

He would say: "Jesus was the only baby born to die!"

Everyone loved Skip, and I think at least two of the older single women at church wish they'd married him!

Skip gave me a simple pattern to follow, which I still use today. He told me, first, to get people to put their trust in God — **to look up** and acknowledge their need of him. Secondly, to **look back** and honour and remember the person who had died. Finally, to **look forward** and consider our own lives and faith as we move on.

I have taken many funerals over the years and still find Skip's simple structure a helpful tool to hang my thoughts on to bring comfort and hope to those suffering grief, loss and sudden loneliness. I was so nervous at my first funeral that I went to say the undertaker's name at the committal instead of the person who had died!

A dear family, who I have known for many years, asked if I would scatter the ashes of their dad. They wanted it done on Farthing Downs in Surrey. I said a few words, opened the box and scattered the ashes in an arc shape as a gust of wind blew some of the ashes back over me. I stood there brushing Alan Hawkins off my best suit trying not to let the family see what I had done.

I like to find out about the person who has died and personalise the message appropriately. Once, I took a funeral of a lady who was really into bingo and had to stop myself from declaring that her number was up!

My most memorable story was at a cremation. The family had chosen contemporary music to be played at the beginning and at the time of the committal when the curtains closed. They were all on a CD and ready to be played. My message that day was that we are all like letters addressed to God. The letter is what is important; it is placed into an envelope and posted on its journey. When it arrives, the envelope is discarded, and the letter is read. I explained that our bodies are like that envelope, but the real us is the letter that goes before God at our final destination. After sharing my letter story, I pushed the button and the curtains started to close and the music began to play.

At the end of the song and before we had time to leave, another track sung by Elvis Presley burst into play:

"Return to sender, address unknown. No such person, no such zone."

I didn't know where to look or what to say, but managed to hold myself together. My eyes caught the glance of another man among the mourners, and he grinned.

I have been reprimanded before by the attendant at a local crematorium for going over my allotted time and hate the thought of having to rush such a personal and poignant occasion.

People tell me that I 'do a good funeral' and a special friend of mine, who is the Headteacher at our favourite school, has pre-booked me to do hers – should she go first!

KEVIN VICKERS

Chapter 24

When Jesus Receives
An Injunction

Mike did his theological training at Birmingham Bible Institute and his first church was in Weaverham, Cheshire. Unlike our background at the Mission, which was traditionally conservative, Mike's training and environment opened him up to embrace a more charismatic side of Christianity. Mike has a pioneering gift and gathers people around him easily. Over the years, he has been able to start new things, some from scratch, because of this gift. We would talk and encourage one another from a distance but always believed we'd work together too. Mike with his apostolic and missionary zeal and me with my pastoral abilities. We thought we'd make a good team.

After several years Mike moved back to Mitcham and planted a church on the Phipps Bridge Estate, called Mitcham Revival Church. He was also given a position on the leadership of Gladstone Mission where I was now acting Pastor and became part of the team of elders with me, Dave and George. The Mission supported Mike's work and whilst it was very different in form and style, it came to be seen as an 'unofficial church plant' of the Mission, led by Mike with some input from me. Mike is very good at mobilising people to do extraordinary things for the gospel. We would prayer walk the entire boundary of Mitcham identifying the twelve gateways into the town.

At each gateway we knocked a six-foot stake into the ground with scripture texts bound around them. For six months we would pray at these junctions for the people of Mitcham. On another occasion, we hand delivered twenty-eight thousand paperback books called 2 Pork Chops to every home in Mitcham. The book was written by a friend of Mike's, called John Masters, and aimed at leading people to Christ.

It was a few years after this time that we decided to host the travelling evangelistic show, Heaven's Gates & Hell's Flames. This is a powerful, dramatic live presentation of the gospel message using drama, multimedia and an incredible stage set. Our people would be trained to do the drama and perform the show over Easter in April 2003. It would take place in a big tent on the Three Kings Piece, in Mitcham, and we'd invite everyone to come.

The problem was our local authority, the London Borough of Merton, didn't want us to do it and wouldn't give us the permission to go ahead. It had been widely publicised, and all our preparations had been made. The tent was booked, we'd hired a generator, chairs and security fencing for the perimeter. Our church members were the cast and had been trained to perform the drama sequences in the show. We were convinced that God wanted this to go ahead, so Mike and I boldly went to Crown House, in Morden, and sought an audience with the lady from the council in the Outside Events Department. I cringe now as I recall this meeting, but we were zealous and passionate about Mitcham hearing the good news of the gospel and saw this lady as standing in our way. We warned her like Moses and Aaron did before the Pharoah of Egypt at the time of the Exodus.

We told her not to stand in the way of what God was doing. She listened to us, and we left.

We checked out local bylaws and didn't think the council had the right to stop us, so we decided to go ahead anyway. Without a key, it meant that we had to lift the gate on the common to drive our vehicles on to get everything ready.

I was playing the part of Jesus and had gone without shaving for three months to grow a small beard. My hair was greying so for the first and only time, I dyed it black. Mike was playing the part of the devil. Everything was ready: Mike and I were in full costumes and people were arriving for the show. Suddenly, a fast car arrived on the scene and a man jumped out and handed us a brown A4 envelope. We opened it to find legal papers from the local authority. Jesus and the devil had both been served an injunction by Merton Council prohibiting us, individually and the church corporately, from being on the common. The injunction was in the names of Kevin and Michael Vickers and All Nations Revival Church, which was now the new name of our church.

We did comply and moved the show to our church building for the Easter period. I can't remember how long the injunction lasted but I can recall, just after walking past the Three Kings Piece and in defiance to the order, putting my foot on the grass verge and taking it off again! I wondered what was being said about us behind closed doors in the council and what kind of crazy church they thought we were.

It would be six years later, and under slightly different circumstances, that I would once again meet the lady from the Outside Events Department of Merton Council.

Chapter 25
Things I'd Change if I Could

I had always been in Mitcham at the Mission, but Mike had moved away and come back. He had experienced church life in other places and returned with new ideas and fresh expressions of worship and evangelism. Mitcham Revival Church on the Phipps Bridge Estate was growing, and new people were joining and becoming Christians. They seemed to enjoy a freedom in the Holy Spirit that was new to the rest of us, and this attracted some of our people over. As Mike was now also on the leadership at the Mission, the two of us had a lot of influence over the others and pushed for change.

I love to tell the story of David the shepherd boy being chosen and anointed as the future King over Israel. His anointing would not be his appointing. David would not force his way to the crown but wait for God's positioning and timing. He would go back to the sheep and wait for God to work things out. I wish I had done that, too. Now, I can see that at times I pushed myself forward and made things happen instead of waiting.

Dave was treated badly by us as we pushed ahead with changes that we thought would usher in the revival we so wanted to see. We loved God and had faith and passion but didn't always act with love and wisdom. Those who opposed us were seen as quenching what God wanted to do. It was at this time that we amalgamated the Mission with Mitcham Revival Church, thereby making one church.

The name was changed to All Nations Revival Church, chosen to reflect the growing multicultural mix of our community. Our meetings became more charismatic and experienced a freedom of expression in worship that some were not used to. On one hand there was great expectancy and excitement for the future, but on the other, there was tension and opposition to change.

Dave was asked to step down and George was deeply troubled and hurt. The church suffered a bereavement, and the Mission lost its identity. There was unrest among many of the old members. Some left and moved churches, others embraced the new thing and stayed. Dave had remarried after his first wife Pat died of cancer and had moved to Morden. His young family would join the local Baptist church. Over the course of the next two years, George and Crystal would move away to be closer to family and others would leave. Lifelong relationships with people who had always been in my life would be broken. The church that is supposed to be modelled on love and unity suffered division, hurt, confusion and unforgiveness. That was not our finest hour.

Things I know now that I didn't really know then:

- Loud music isn't more spiritual than quiet music.

- New songs are not necessarily better than old hymns and choruses – both can be good.

- You don't need a worship band at the front of the church, although it can be nice.

- Sometimes people will use spiritual jargon to do what they want to do.

- Some so-called spiritual experiences are because of learnt behaviour.

- Even in church, people follow personalities.

- Things are not always what they seem.

- Love is greater than faith, but faith working through love is essential.

- I hurt people who nurtured and loved me.

I thank God for his grace and forgiveness, and that even after all this God in his sovereignty can still 'make all things work together for good to those who love him'. I hope and pray that all those who are still hurting will find it in their hearts to extend forgiveness too.

Maybe this book will help...

KEVIN VICKERS

Chapter 26

Strapping on our Swords

Mike and I were now joint Pastors of All Nations Revival Church. The church was growing, and we had moved from the chapel into the main hall. Mel Gibson's 'The Passion of the Christ' was about to be released in cinemas across the country, and Christians saw this as a major evangelistic opportunity. I contacted Streatham Odeon and got permission for us to have a table in their foyer with tracts and follow-up material for those who had been moved by the film. We manned this with people from church every afternoon and evening for two weeks. I also got permission to jump up and address the audience for a couple of minutes at the end of the film in the evenings. It was agreed that they'd cut the credits and raise the lights so people could see me. It was scary and sometimes I got booed, but some people listened.

On one occasion someone complained to the manager that the credits had been cut. Apparently, they were part of the production team and wanted to see their name in lights. Instead, they saw me. This was the last time I was allowed to speak at the cinema.

That same year, in June 2004, a London-wide outreach, called Soul in the City, took place. I was keen for the churches in Mitcham to unite and work together, and can remember being part of a planning meeting at Mitcham Methodist Church.

Among other things, we wanted to hire a massive stage and host the World Wide Message Tribe, a Christian dance band from Manchester, which was quite famous at the time among young people. We had £18,000 to find, which looked totally out of our reach. I challenged everyone around the table that, as leaders, it was our responsibility to give first. Immediately, a lady at the end of the table passed up an envelope with £500 cash in it. The money was from a car sale earlier that day; she had it in her bag and felt prompted to give. Cheque books came out and others followed suit. We raised enough at that meeting for the first instalment to be paid and the rest of the money came in when needed. Soul in the City was a great community event and a faith-building exercise for the church working together.

The Shaftesbury Society was our official landlord, but there was no formal financial agreement between us. The building at 'Gladstone Mission' legally belonged to them and on the 12th April, 2005, Mike and I were called to a meeting at their offices in south Wimbledon. The meeting was with the Company Secretary, Mike Langworth. He informed us that Shaftesbury were to sell the Mission on the open market and that we needed to vacate the premises by the 30th September, 2005. Of course, we were shocked and began to plan our defence. Over the next four weeks, we built our case.

I had a friend who was a Christian solicitor who helped us write a response and claim our rights as sitting tenants. It was the 9th May, and I can still remember walking to the post box on Haslemere Avenue to post the letter. As I got close, I heard the words, "You've strapped on your swords." I knew exactly what that meant, and I also knew that that was the voice of God to my conscience. I never posted the letter, instead I ripped it up and returned home.

There's a passage in the Bible where David and his men plan to take revenge on a wealthy, yet foolish landowner, who had refused them charity. David says to his men, "Strap on your swords", and they set out for retribution. Nabal's wife Abigail learns about this and intercepts David before he gets there. With great wisdom and insight, she pleads with David in front of his six hundred men not to avenge himself but to leave it with God. David humbles himself and admits that she is right. I knew that God wanted us to do the same: to leave it with him and not fight. I called Mike and told him, and he agreed too.

That same day, I wrote another letter to Mike Langworth at the Shaftesbury Society. I told him that we would comply with their request to leave the building in Love Lane on the 30th September – and we did.

KEVIN VICKERS

Chapter 27

Doing "Church" Differently

Sometimes when we're on holiday, Jane might say, "Look at that lovely church!" I would always reply, "That's not a church, it's a church building!" Then she thumps me because we both know that - it's just what we say! Not everyone knows that, though. The truth is the church is the people, not the buildings. If only we would value and invest as much time, money and energy in people as we do buildings.

On the 2nd October, 2005, All Nations Revival Church moved into Cricket Green School, in Mitcham, and have been part of the school community ever since. But when I stood at the front on that first Sunday morning, after we'd left our buildings in Love Lane, I wouldn't be truthful if I didn't admit feeling a little heartsick. I knew the church wasn't the building, but at that moment I wished I could have the building back. Nevertheless, I knew deep down that this was our time for doing 'church' differently, so we embraced the challenge with both hands.

We experimented with holding church in homes on Sunday mornings and this worked for a while, particularly in the summer months, but we would eventually return to Cricket Green School and make it our permanent home.

Our church office ran out of Toomey Estate Agents in Mitcham, thanks to Kim, mum of Hayley, one of our church members. Kim gave me my own desk, phone line and storage for church office equipment.

I had a key and access to office space and printing and fax facilities.

I had the honour of praying a blessing at the opening of their second shop in Tooting Junction. Kim could not do enough for us at that time, and we remain massively grateful.

In the summer of 2005, Jane and Hayley attended a meeting in Sutton and got introduced to the growing work of Street Pastors. Street Pastors is the church on the streets, generally late at night, listening, caring and helping. Not one church, but individuals from churches working together, and in partnership with the local authority and the police. Not overtly preaching but being light and salt and a calming influence for peace and good.

Jane and Hayley were full of it when they returned, and this led to several of our church members training to become Street Pastors in Mitcham, at the same time that we were vacating our building in Love Lane. It would be later reported at a Churches Together in Mitcham meeting that All Nations Revival Church was closing and all their members were becoming Street Pastors! Not exactly...

Our base for the first Mitcham Street Pastor Team was, of course, Toomey Estate Agents.

Doing church differently means for us that we must set everything up and pack everything away afterwards. Our advertising and promotion must be tailored carefully and our communication relevant. For several years, we were using temporary banners on the fence outside the school over the weekends. But now we have permanent signage outside the school gates. When we first did this my daughter, Rachel, Photoshopped the sign so that it read:

All Nations Revival Church

Also meeting here:

Cricket Green School

We sent it to the Headteacher, who has become a friend, saying: "Is this okay?" We are so grateful for the amazing relationship that we enjoy with the school and ways in which we partner together for the benefit of the community.

We are a church prepared to take risks, you've probably guessed that already. What I mean is our projects are not money-driven but people-centred. If a need comes across our door, we will look for ways of meeting it. We are a 'can do' church.

In the Old Testament, God led his people through the wilderness with a cloud by day and a pillar of fire by night. They lived in tents and would be ready at a moment's notice to strike camp and move on if the cloud moved. I believe the church should be that spontaneous and obedient today. I call it 'tent mentality'.

Our relationships with other evangelical, charismatic Bible believing churches are important. We are grateful to be in covenant relationship with Kingdom Faith in Horsham, and subscribe to the Evangelical Alliance's Statement of Faith. This accountability is vital and healthy to stay true to our beliefs and not lose our way.

There are many churches today that 'do church differently', so we are far from alone. I want to finish where I started. Buildings are good and necessary, but they are not the church.

The church is the people!

Chapter 28

Advancing Through the Tough Times

When my children were at middle school, I attended their sports day and entered the parents race at the end. It was the 100 metres sprint and I thought I had a good chance of winning. The trouble was I was wearing shoes and the grass was wet. Still secretly smug, I lined up with the others and was about to show off when Mr Hyde fired the pistol, and the race began. Immediately, I slipped on my face as all the other parents sped off. I managed to regain my composure and race after them. I didn't come last, but even Mark Pickett beat me, and I was sure I could run faster than him!

As a boy, I'd attended this same school and had my sports day on the same field. I was better at long distance running!

The Bible has a lot to say about endurance and perseverance. Many start, but not everyone finishes well. I want to finish well and take others with me. Life is not a short sprint but a marathon. Because church is doing life together, it also has its ups and downs, good times, bad times, exciting times and tough times. We would have our fair share of these!

Over the following three years, Mike and I developed new things both in the church and in the community. Mike produced and led a forty day discipleship programme for men, called 'Boot Camp', that became popular with other churches.

He also did a National Walk of Witness from Thurso, in Scotland, to Brighton, on the south coast, carrying what we called the Kingdom Flag. He was sharing the gospel, handing out tracts, and praying for people on the way. This would lead to the birth of Cross the Nations, an international ministry largely in Europe, where Mike would walk across cities carrying a cross and sharing the gospel.

As well as the regular pastoral work at All Nations Revival Church, I was spending some of my time teaching the Bible in local primary schools. I was also co-ordinating the development of Merton Street Pastors across the borough and, through a friend, had been introduced to the International Leadership Institute. I didn't know it then, but this would open for me the opportunity to teach a leadership training programme for young and emerging leaders throughout Europe.

In 2009, Mike stepped down from leadership at our church to pursue his 'Crosswalks' and, eventually, the family moved back to Cheshire, where they took up the reins of the church again in Weaverham. I was now the sole pastor of All Nations Revival Church and my leadership was not as charismatic as my brother's. Over time, some people followed Mike and Sarah to Cheshire and others moved on. It was a hard time for me and Jane, and difficult not to take it personally. But we are overcomers, and our faith kept us going!

Our numbers dropped and there was a time when we had no musicians at the front of the church. Sundays could be my hardest and most discouraging day.

The other things I was doing in the community and abroad were thriving and helped me keep going during this time. The church was being refined and renewed and eventually new people began to join, and those that stayed stepped up and took on new responsibilities. I matured as a leader and came to appreciate some of the profound ways of God. We would come out of a wilderness period stronger, wiser and more passionate for the deeper things of God. It was also during this time that Jon had his accident in America and the church pulled together to support us.

I would often compare myself to Mike and feel inadequate, but Mike has said he sometimes compares himself to me and feels the same. How ridiculous, because we are different and that's okay! I wonder whether Joshua felt inadequate following in the footsteps of Moses. God had to remind him that Moses was no more and that this was his time to lead. All he needed to know was, "As I was with Moses, so I will be with you; I will never leave you nor forsake you." *Joshua 1:5 (NIV)*. I knew this was true for me, too, I just didn't always feel it!

I get to teach a lot on leadership and yet I am still learning all the time. I know it requires strength and courage. The joy of the Lord is my strength, and my courage is drawn from my faith in Christ. I also know that fear and discouragement are my enemies to overcome. Fear wants to paralyse and stop me from going forward, and discouragement wants to rip out my heart and say, "What's the point?"

I'll have none of that! God called Joshua to advance in flood times and Isaac planted in a year of famine and reaped one hundredfold because God nourished the seed. Jesus said,

> *"In this world you will have trouble. But take heart! I have overcome the world."*

> **John 16:33 (NIV)**

Light always overcomes darkness and the Church is the light of the world.

I have also learnt that it is not 'my' church, or 'my brother's' church but God's church.

Jesus said,

> *"I will build my church, and the gates of hell will not overcome it."*

> **Matthew 16:18 (NIV)**

Pressure off!

GOBSMACKED

KEVIN VICKERS

GOBSMACKED
IN SCHOOLS

KEVIN VICKERS

Chapter 29

My First Assembly - Not my Finest Hour!

I was eighteen and a new Christian and hadn't yet learnt what was appropriate and what wasn't. I left school at sixteen and had taken a morning off work from the bank to lead a school assembly at my old high school, Eastfields in Mitcham. A group of us from the Mission had put together a drama about the woman caught in adultery. We wanted to create a surprise element, so we had members of the cast in the audience sitting among the students.

I stood up, dressed in a suit and tie, and walked to the lectern with my Bible. I opened it and with a loud voice and a thump on the lectern for affect, began to read from the old English King James Version. You could feel the tension rise in the room among the teachers, who must have been thinking, "What on earth is going on?" Suddenly, on cue, one of our team started to shout from the floor, having a go at me for preaching in such a judgemental way. This was the introduction to our little sketch. Ros was then dragged onto the stage as the adulteress, and someone played the part of Jesus. Eventually we got to the bit where Jesus says: "If anyone of you is without sin, let him be the first to throw a stone at her," and so it went on.

We never got invited back.

I was a bit older, now, and got invited back to Liberty Middle School to do an assembly for the second or third time. Mr King was the Headteacher and Mr Hyde was his deputy. This time, I took a friend with me called Mary Renton. My assembly was about the Lord's Prayer. I would read a line and Mary (who was hidden away), would play the part of God and answer me so that there was a kind of dialogue going on. My point was that prayer is a two-way thing. Apparently, Mr King did not like that assembly, and I never got invited back. Despite my phone calls to the school, I could never get through to Mr King.

It would be several years later, when my own children attended Liberty Middle School, that we would have an honest and frank conversation about the assembly. After that meeting, he allowed me back in and would later invite me to join the governing body of the school.

I have remained friends with both Chris King and Paul Hyde since their retirement. Over the years, we have shared a curry together with other colleagues. I've tried to support and be a listening ear to Chris after his eldest son died during the Covid pandemic.

It's good to talk things out – deeper friendships and other good things can come from it.

Chapter 30
Fuzzy-Felt Man

I love visual aids and will use them when I am teaching children and adults alike. I believe Jesus used visual aids when he taught. He just didn't need to carry them around with him in a big bag, like I do. Instead, he pointed at the birds, or the flowers, or the farmer, or the shepherd, or the rocks, or the thorns, or the mountains...

I love telling Bible stories to children in primary schools and find the best way to do it is with my old fashioned Fuzzy-Felt board. I came across 'Betty Lukens flannelgraph', or felt board, twenty-six years ago when I was with my friend and co-worker Peter Kendrick. He had one set up all ready to go. Peter ran the Schools Christian Resource Centre in Morden, and once a month we would meet with others to pray for children in our schools. Peter has a well-known brother, Graham, who is a worship leader and songwriter, famous for writing 'Shine Jesus Shine' among other songs sung in churches today.

I persuaded the leaders at the Mission to buy me one from America. What I didn't realise was that it comes in large sheets of felt with hundreds of pieces to be individually cut out. Pauline, who ran the Girls Brigade, took the lead on this along with some other ladies. Each numbered piece was then carefully placed into the box on cardboard sheets marked out with the correct shape accordingly.

It was an art and a science! It also came with three main backgrounds: sky and sea, night-time and indoors, already mounted on thick cardboard designed to be folded in half for storage. Other scenery is then added, such as trees, shrubs and mountains as required. Over the years, I have become quite an expert at gathering the right pieces together and knowing what goes where. It wasn't that easy in the beginning.

I also call it my retro board. In the high-tech age in which we live, my 'flannelgraph' can be a real novelty for keeping the children's attention for twenty minutes in an assembly. Most of them have never seen anything like it before. I get called all sorts of names by the children such as, The Fuzzy-Felt Man, The Man from Bethlehem or The Jesus Man. I'm not sure what the staff call me behind my back! After visiting Mitcham primary schools for so long, occasionally a staff member will tell me that they remember when I used to come to their school when they were a child.

I was taking an Easter assembly at Cricket Green Special School once and was setting up my board with the key people for the story, when the children came filing in. Suddenly, a little boy broke loose of his teacher, ran over to my picture board, and ran off with Jesus. I was about to start but had lost my main character! The children are always fascinated at how the pieces stick on the board. Sometimes, I will choose one or two of them to help me. I used to go into my children's schools, too. They were excited about me coming in when they were at their first school, Harland, but when I started coming to Liberty Middle, they weren't so keen. "Dad," they'd say, "don't wear those trainers, they're embarrassing."

The flannelgraph also comes in handy when we take short services in care and nursing homes in Mitcham. It gives the residents a focal point and helps to keep their attention. Last Christmas, we organised carol singing, readings, and Christmas storytelling in the White Lion of Mortimer pub. The DJ set up spotlights for my board and let us use his microphones. During the lockdown of Covid-19, I decided to video key stories on my iPad all the way through the Bible. I started with Creation and finished with Revelation, when Jesus returns. Every week, I filmed a different story on the flannelgraph for about fifteen minutes and posted it on YouTube and Facebook. I hope they will be a resource for churches and a legacy for my grandchildren.

I have a spare flannelgraph now, but the quality is not the same. My old one is a bit worn and Jesus has seen better days, but I'm sticking with the original for as long as I can. We gifted a whole new flannelgraph set to the True Gospel Harvest Mission in Wellington, Sierra Leone, a few years ago. Sadly, when I revisited, they had not taken it out of the box. We then spent a whole afternoon cutting the felt and positioning the pieces. I did some training with the leaders and encouraged them to use it. I hope and pray that they too will find their Fuzzy-Felt board to be a rich resource for bringing Bible stories to life, just as I have.

KEVIN VICKERS

Chapter 31

When a Chance Meeting Affects a Lifetime

It was May 1995, and I was working part-time for NatWest as the Assistant Manager at Clapham Common branch. It was then that I decided to attend the annual Christian Resources Exhibition at Sandown Park racecourse for the first time.

The CRE, as it's usually called, is a one-stop shop for suppliers to the church scene to show off, promote, and sell their wares. Running over four days, and set over three floors, you could buy anything from Communion wine to a vicar's shirt. You could talk to missionaries and apply for Bible college. There were resources for children's work, youth work and sermon outlines, plus so much more. As well as a host of Christian organisations promoting their work, there were also 'taster' seminars going on at different times during the day. It felt a bit like Christmas in May. So much to see, I didn't know where to start. I was on the top floor and accidentally wandered into a room just as a seminar was about to start.

Cliff Keeys was the UK Director of Walk Through the Bible, a ministry that he'd started with his wife in 1984 after being trained in the USA. They taught the 'Big Picture' of the Bible in a fun, interactive and memorable way using keywords and hand signs that brought the Bible to life.

Cliff turned the room into a map and 'walked us through' the key events, key people and the key places of the Bible in a chronological way.

Cliff was from Sunderland, and he won me over with his accent, humour and storytelling. The seminar introduced a new children's version they'd developed called Bible Explorer. It would be taught in the same fun way but was aimed at storytelling through the Bible for nine- to eleven- year- olds in primary schools. They were recruiting people to be trained as part of a national team to teach this programme in local schools as part of the work of the church. I loved it from the word go. I knew that this was no chance meeting but a defining moment in my life. I signed up for the training immediately and have never looked back. 'Bible Explorer' would become a strategic resource for sowing the knowledge of the Bible into the lives of many children in my town, rather than just the few who attended Sunday school.

As Bible Explorer was designed as an educational resource for schools, I was not allowed to teach it at church. I understood the integrity of this rule, and schools welcomed it to complement their own R.E. syllabus. Over the years in Mitcham, Morden and Wimbledon, I was able to train up a local team of presenters to teach in more than twenty Merton schools, including one special school. It would all be voluntary and grew through trust and relationships with school staff. The children are taught for one hour every week for five weeks to cover the Old Testament, and the same with the New Testament. One Testament fits in nicely to half a school term.

Unlike when I was at school, the children are usually looking forward with excitement to their R.E. lesson!

Once, I was teaching a whole year group at Gorringe Park Middle School, with five classes together in the hall. I was teaching the ten plagues, and when I got to the plague of locusts, I shouted and threw a rubber locust into the crowd of children. The head of Year 5 screamed and ran out of the hall. I thought I would get into trouble for that but survived to teach another day! Another time, I was teaching a year group in St Thomas of Canterbury RC School, and there was a trainee teacher in the class. It seemed to be going well when I asked a question and, suddenly, the teacher burst out with the answer. I think she'd got so caught up in the lesson that she forgot she was the teacher. A bit embarrassed, she put her hand to her mouth and the rest of us laughed.

I had no formal training to teach, so I learnt on the job. I also learnt some behaviour management techniques from others. The children would often get excited, but I could usually keep their attention when I needed to. It was important for a member of staff to always be in my lessons, and sometimes they would calm the children down when they got excited. Once, I had a teaching assistant who was constantly telling the children off and interrupting my lesson. Afterwards, the Headteacher, who was a friend of mine, asked me how the lesson went. I told her it was going great except for one problem: the teaching assistant. The following week I had a different staff member in my class, and everything was fine.

My friend, Steve, was the vicar at St Mark's Church in Mitcham, and part of our school's team. He tells the story of teaching at one school where there was a boy in the class called Gospel. Apparently, he was definitely NOT good news!

I was training Caroline on the job once, and it was her turn to teach. We turned up at the school, and on the way in, the teacher said, "Good luck, you have the class from hell" (or something similar). I laughed as Caroline's face fell. It turned out that they were fine, and Caroline did great. I am still passionate about teaching 'Bible Explorer'; although the name has changed, the concept remains the same. I regularly meet ex-pupils of all ages who remember the lessons. Once, I was queuing in KFC when a young lady turned to me and said, "I remember you; you came to my school!" And then, in front of all the other customers, shouted, "Transfiguration," and made the hand sign I'd taught her back then.

In 2011 and 2013, I'd train to teach Walk Through the Bible adult seminars and even more opportunities would open for me. Every year since that first visit, I have regularly attended the Christian Resources Exhibition at Sandown Park, just in case I accidentally find another 'defining moment' in my life!

Chapter 32
It's Not What You Know, its.....

It's not what you know, it's **who** you know. This is a phrase I often use. I believe it's true, but it starts with knowing God! My inward peace, value, security and identity are all found in knowing the one who intimately knows and cares for me. I can have full confidence that my life and future are not a result of chance or luck, but guided and led by my Heavenly Father. My relationship with God, through Christ, is by far the most important one and ultimately influences all the others.

Being a church leader, I have come to value and esteem my relationships outside of church. There's an old saying, "You can be too heavenly minded to be any earthly good." I don't believe that! But I know what people mean, and I don't want to be one of them.

Peter Kendrick used to produce a list of 'schools workers' with a short pen picture of each as an introduction for schools. It was a kind of accreditation or reference that this person wasn't going to start preaching in class or making altar calls in assembly. Sometimes, this would happen with a zealous young evangelist, and the school would close the door to all schools workers, tarnishing us with the same brush.

For me it is about trust over time and building good relationships.

As I look back over the years, I am grateful for the trust and opportunities I have been given to be part of the wider community. I remember being invited every Christmas to the children's nativity at Malmesbury Primary School, in Morden. I would attend a special reception with the governors in the Headteacher's office before the show began. Sometimes, I get invited to staff leaving dos or special celebration assemblies. I have also had the privilege of writing references for some of my school colleague friends when they've moved jobs. When I've wanted to get into a particular school but couldn't get past the receptionist, I've asked for an introduction from someone who knows them. Peta, the Headteacher at Morden Primary, once asked me if there were any local schools that we were not teaching 'Bible Explorer' in. I made a list and she emailed all of them to recommend us. I had first met Peta at Cranmer Primary and followed her to Morden. My youngest son, Jon, would also complete his teacher training at Morden School.

I got to know Despo at Cranmer when she was head of Year 6, and would follow her to Bond Primary, where she was the deputy and later became the head. Despo had such a love and passion for the children that she would go the extra mile and get involved in their lives and families. When she retired in 2019, she would adopt three children associated with her school whose mother was killed in a road accident. I would regularly pop into Bond to see Despo and I would pray with her for the children; she loved all of them, particularly the difficult ones. She would host termly prayer meetings for us in the school after hours for other staff to join.

They were precious times. She would also introduce me to the delights of red wine!

As a church leader and friend of schools, I may be asked to give pastoral support in times of crises or tragedy, and offer words of comfort and hope to those who are suffering. Often this is just being available to listen.

Perhaps one of my greatest honours was to receive a telephone call from Neena. Neena was the new head of an Independent Islamic school in Mitcham, and she called to ask if I would come and teach Bible Explorer to the older children in her school as part of the curriculum. I have known Neena since her time at Cranmer primary and was overwhelmed by her trust in me to teach her children. I had never taught in a Muslim school before but being given the opportunity was humbling.

When I was a Small Business Adviser, I learnt that people generally do business with people they trust. I believe that this is also a foundation for deep and lasting relationships. I am richer because of the relationships I enjoy; I hope you are too.

KEVIN VICKERS

Chapter 33
Wearing Different Hats

I was driving home from Croydon and passing Croydon Cemetery when my mobile phone rang. I pulled over and spoke to Paul Williams, one of the senior leaders at Cricket Green School, who asked if I could help them run a mini-enterprise scheme for the older children at the school. As I often do, I said yes and would work out the finer details later.

I would be the bank manager and set up a mock NatWest Bank at the school. The children would come to me in small groups, and I would interview them about their enterprising ideas for making a profit at the school summer fair. I would lend them small amounts of money, and they would have to pay the loans back with interest. It was a lot of fun and a great learning experience. This was a school where I would also take assemblies. One day, one of the children met me in the corridor and asked, "Kevin, are you the bank manager or the vicar today?" I answered, "Both!"

A few years later, I was part of the same project at Bond with Despo and her team. The children would come into my office with their business plans, and I would scrutinise them for the detail. I loaned them money from the bank for materials and cashflow and attended the school fair, where each group had their own stall. I think I helped them all make a profit that day by buying a load of stuff!

When our first son, Samuel, was born, Jane gave up banking and was a stay-at-home mum until all three of our children were old enough to go to school. She did small cleaning jobs that helped pay the bills and finally, in January 1997, got a part-time teaching assistant post at Cricket Green Special School. This soon became a full-time position and would later help pave the way for the school to become our church home. Twenty-five years on, and Jane is still there, as a family support worker.

The finance officer at Cranmer School asked me one day if I'd do an audit or independent check of their school fund account. I agreed, and later the school gave me a donation for my work. She asked me if I wouldn't mind her passing my name on to a colleague in another school. I said that would be fine, so she did, and I had two school funds to audit. Word spread and over the years I have accumulated some twenty-five schools who have asked me to help with their audits. I've had to start invoicing for the work, and now have to do a tax return for the extra income I receive! *Gobsmacked!* The Lord provides!

Another hat I would come to wear would be that of a school governor!

Chapter 34

School Governor

It was in the school year of 2002/03 that I first became a governor at Cricket Green School. Celia Dawson was the new Headteacher, and she came with a vision to challenge stereotypes, champion inclusion, and push the boundaries of special education to a new place. It was a good time to join, even though I knew nothing of what it involved, and had to learn a new internal language of school acronyms and jargon.

My family would come to love the heartbeat of special education and two of our children would later work at the school. It was a steep learning curve being a governor, and I used to say that I was making it up as I was going along but then I say that about most things. It's not completely true but there is a truth in it. I remember when I was Assistant Manager (Lending) at NatWest Tooting, where I'd sit in my office listening to business propositions. I'd learn to nod and comment in the right places but sometimes I'd be thinking, "I don't understand what you are talking about!" I'd learn to trust my instincts and usually the mist cleared, so I'd know how to proceed, but it was scary at times.

My colleagues on the governing body were great people and seemed very experienced. They were there because they cared about the school and its community, and wanted to make a difference in the lives of the children. Glyne was the chair and Nick Draper was the local authority governor representative.

Nick has a son with special educational needs living in residential care and was totally committed to his role at the school.

I also remember Michael Darby, a parent governor with a son at Cricket Green who led the fight to keep the school open when some wanted special schools to close. Michael was very articulate, passionately persistent, but also soft hearted. I affectionately nicknamed him the 'naughty governor' after getting to know him.

Steve Goodwin was also part of the governing body at that time and his family were heavily involved in organising social activities and running the Parent Teacher Association. I was there as a community representative and hoped to be able to add value too. I was assigned to the finance committee because of my banking background, and the personnel committee seemed to be a good fit with my pastoral abilities. A few years passed and, somehow, I became chair of governors, with Nick as the vice chair. It has been like this for sixteen years. We are fortunate to have an incredibly experienced and committed governing body who get on well together and are fully involved in the life of the school.

I have always seen my main role as pastoral, and over the years, I have used it to support Celia, her staff, children and families wherever I can. When our church moved in, we became a trusted extension of the school community and have often been able to provide practical help, pastoral support and prayer, where appropriate.

This has included budget and debt counselling, cleaning, befriending, bereavement support, counselling and, among other things, form-filling. I had the privilege of giving a eulogy at Nick's wife's funeral and praying with Celia and her father before he died. Celia has become a close friend of our family and will always remain so.

The 'Leavers Assembly' has always been a tearjerker at the end of term. I get the opportunity to say a few words of encouragement as the Year 11's move on to new things or further their education in 6th form or college. Each child is celebrated for who they are and what they've achieved. Not primarily in academic qualifications, but in character, resilience, independence and life skills. Every small step is recognised and cheered.

I was in a meeting once with Celia and a group of primary Headteachers from mainstream schools. We were going around the table introducing ourselves when it came to my turn. Without thinking I said, "I'm Kevin Vickers, the Headteacher of Cricket Green School". Celia was sitting opposite me, and I could see confusion on her face. Eventually she said, "No you're not, I am!" Everyone laughed out loud. I can still see Celia's face thinking, "Is he?"

For a while, I was also on the governing body of Liberty Primary, where Chris King was head. My friend, the Rev Steve Coulson, was also a member and we used to joke about him having two vicars on his board. There came a time where I felt I needed to review my outside commitments, and this was one I decided to step down from.

The Cricket Green School community plays a massive part in my life, family and church. Our flexible rental terms remind me of a children's TV show when I was a boy called, 'Andy Pandy and Looby Loo'. Looby Loo would come out when Andy Pandy was asleep and get up to all sorts of things. I am sure Mrs Dawson has no idea what we get up to at church when she's not around! Only good stuff, of course.

And, just like NatWest in Wimbledon, Jane is the keyholder. I'm *Gobsmacked* at how things work out sometimes!

Chapter 35

Becoming a Bus Driver

In **Philippians 4:13**, it says,

> *"I can do everything through him who gives me strength."* Well, I never expected to become a bus driver!

In January 2008, I wrote to the Souter Trust in Perth with plans for our community project, which involved a double-decker bus. We were asking if the charity would provide us with a second-hand bus that we could convert for use in schools and our local community. They did!

That summer, Jane and I, along with Rev Steve and my friend Armstrong, the vicar of Mitcham Methodist Church, travelled to Perth in Scotland to choose our bus. We would stay overnight with a vicar friend called Robert Pickles. We arrived at his manse before he was home, but he had told us where the key was to get in. I thought it would be fun to explore the big house, so I sent Armstrong upstairs to look. He opened the door to a bedroom and was about to walk in when he saw someone asleep in the bed. The person never woke up as Armstrong quietly closed the door and crept back downstairs. We laughed so much, we felt like naughty schoolchildren.

The following day we attended the Stagecoach depot and were allowed to choose our bus.

They asked us what colour we wanted them to spray it, and they agreed to remove all the seats.

We decided on navy blue, my favourite colour! Jane would be the designer and work on the conversion plans, and a few weeks later, Steve would make the trip back up to Scotland with a bus driver, who was a member of his congregation, to drive our bus to its new home in Mitcham. It would take them twenty-four hours to get back as the bus wouldn't go any faster than 30 miles per hour, even on the motorways. Steve would try and sleep on the only seat at the back and, en route, would leave the bus at a service station on the M25 to briefly return to Mitcham to conduct a funeral. Later, we discovered that there was a lever in the engine that was in the wrong position. Once moved, the bus drove faster!

The Tooting & Mitcham Hub allowed us to park the bus on their premises while we raised funds for the conversion work. About nine months later, we moved it to the coachworks to begin its conversion into the 'Hope Bus'. It was a faith project to raise the monies totalling £70,000. Downstairs would be a café area with a coffee bar and seating. Upstairs, a classroom area was created, which was carpeted with fold-down tables, mounted TV, and workstations for computers. There was a separate room at the back with a table, chairs and storage for activities and materials. It was sign written on the outside with 'LOVE MITCHAM', our 'Hope Bus' logo, and the words: "Plans to prosper, give Hope and a future worth having..." These words were based on the words from Jeremiah 29:11.

We wanted everyone who saw the bus and encountered it to find hope!

It took a year to complete, and on the 11th June, 2010 it was dedicated to God for its work in Mitcham. The next day, it formed part of the Mitcham Carnival procession, where we opened it up to the community for the first time.

We gathered a Hope Bus team from across different churches and had a small pool of 'proper' bus drivers we could call on. One church member, Hayley, had a relative who was a bus driving instructor at the garage, and she managed to persuade Mario to teach me and Dick to drive the Hope Bus. Although our bus was technically a bus, it was insured as a light goods vehicle because it was no longer carrying passengers. As such, it could be driven under a category on our normal driving licence. And so it was, Dick and I were trained as bus drivers!

Inspired by the film, Pay It Forward, I came up with a whole school project called, Acts of Random Kindness or ARK. The idea was to take the 'Hope Bus' into primary schools and, through song, drama, storytelling, action challenges and video, inspire every child to do acts of random kindness, showing them how they could make a difference for good. Over two to three days, each class would visit the bus for about thirty-five minutes. One of the team would greet them at the door, wearing a bus conductor's hat, and prepare them for their time inside. We had a tight script to work to and a short turnaround time between classes, but it was enormous fun and always well received.

Later we would offer ARK 2, The Power of Words.

We would run the ARK projects in many schools over the years, and every time it would be an adventure. It would be in preparing for one of these outings that Mum would receive some news that she'd waited thirty years to hear.

But that's for a bit later...

GOBSMACKED

KEVIN VICKERS

GOBSMACKED
IN THE COMMUNITY

KEVIN VICKERS

Chapter 36
Ministry to the Margins

Ministry to the Margins was a rubbish name for an outreach we began many years ago, aimed at reaching the most vulnerable in our town. I don't like the word 'ministry' in this context anymore because it sounds like something we were 'doing' to people. It was really more about who we were being among people, whose lives had become severely challenged and disrupted because of drug and alcohol abuse, homelessness and other underlying issues. We wanted to share our lives and the love of God with those who found themselves out there in the margins. And many of these dear people became our friends.

'Baldy Joe' was born and raised in Mitcham and a regular to our group. He loved to play snooker and didn't always take it well when he lost. We had a competition once, and he won, so we made him a certificate and framed it. When I visited his home later, the certificate was in pride of place on his wall. Little things like that meant the world to him. Joe would say he was an alcoholic, and despite stints in rehab, he was never able to complete the time and fully be free of drink. I would often see Joe with his can of lager or cider concealed in a brown paper bag. I might sit with him and share a portion of chips, but he wasn't usually interested in eating much.

There was Clayton – a gently spoken Scot who loved and cared for his dog – Max, Custer, Lisa as well as Alan, Pat, Daniel and Lisa's friend, Elaine. These became our core group.

We met Dave when we were running a joint tent mission with other churches in Mitcham. There was a big marquee in the centre, and Dave was sleeping rough nearby. By the end of the week, he was sleeping inside the tent and, afterwards, we managed to find temporary housing for him while we got to know and befriend him and prepare him for rehab. Dave was addicted to alcohol but was looking for help and wanted to be free. We took Dave and some of the others for a trip to Isabella Plantations in Richmond Park. I was driving my car and Dave was in the front seat next to me with others in the back. Dave started to open up about how he was treated by his father and that he'd never forgive him. Immediately, a well-meaning team member in the back responded by telling Dave that he needed to forgive his dad for his own state of mind. Dave lost it. Shouting and swearing he opened the car door to get out as I was driving. I managed to stop the car and calm the situation, but it was a huge learning curve for our team. It was not the time or place to be talking to Dave about forgiveness. We allowed Dave to sleep at the Mission in one of the rooms for a while. He would turn up about 9pm very drunk, and I would lock him in until the following morning, about 8am, when he would leave. Jackie, who led our team, used to say to me, "What would Crystal say, if she knew what we were doing?" And we would laugh.

GOBSMACKED

Before the days of more stringent health and safety rules and risk assessments, we were quite oblivious and naïve to the risks we took. We were driven by our hearts and sometimes got it wrong, but we were willing to learn.

In November 2006, we took the whole group away for a night to a retreat centre run by my friend, Gail. The centre was at the Torch Trust for the Blind in Hurstpierpoint. We hired a minibus and arranged a time to meet, but because most people hadn't turned up, we went looking for them around Mitcham. We saw Garnet in the street; he was someone I casually knew so we invited him, and he jumped in!

With a full bus of friends, we started our journey to West Sussex. Gail had made it very special for us; everyone had their own room, there was plenty of food, stuff to do and beautiful surroundings to enjoy. Joe decided to sleep in a chair in the main room, most of them didn't want to eat much and one lady – who could be difficult – insisted on us taking her back home.

On our way back, we got a call from the others. Some of the guys wanted us to buy beer and bring it back. I'm not sure if we made the right decision, but we stopped and Hayley went into an off-licence to make the purchase. When we returned, we played snooker and Jenga, and Custer taught us how to balance a fork and spoon on the side of a cup with a matchstick. We had valuable time together, laughed a lot and created memories that were priceless. It was hard work, emotionally demanding, but we'd do it all over again.

I'd like to say that everyone lived happily ever-after but, sadly, that would not be true. Some of our friends are no longer here, others moved away and we lost contact. But some did go on to enjoy a new start in a new place and with a brighter future.

Daniel was one of these.

KEVIN VICKERS

Chapter 37

Street Pastors

Street Pastors is a volunteer Christian franchise that started in 2003 in Brixton. It trains ordinary church members to walk the streets of their towns and cities, usually late at night and into the early morning, listening, caring, and helping. We started Merton Street Pastors after being trained in September 2005, and initially mobilised churches in Mitcham to get involved. It is now a growing registered charity with over forty active volunteers employing a part-time co-ordinator and deploying patrols into Mitcham, Wimbledon and Morden on Friday nights. It has been brilliant for getting the church out of its buildings, into communities and engaging with all kinds of people in the night-time economy. It has also helped Christians from more than forty different church backgrounds, to serve together and respect one another's differences.

Jane and I trained together over twelve Saturdays in Brixton with a hundred others from different London boroughs. It was so exciting to get our uniforms and walk around Mitcham, feeling bold and empowered. I think the uniforms made us braver about talking to people. I remember there were four of us, early on, walking towards a group of young people wearing hoodies. It was late at night and, from a distance, they looked intimidating. We greeted them in a loud friendly way. They put their hoodies down and we had an amazing time sharing and laughing together. How wrong first impressions can be.

We have learnt to be less judgmental and more accepting. We are constantly surprised at the reception we get, and how open and willing people are to tell us very personal things. We always offer to pray, and most people agree. When we first began, I ordered hundreds of wristbands for the team to give away. I love the Johnny English films, with Rowan Atkinson playing a bumbling spy character in the style of James Bond. There's a scene where you see a fake Archbishop of Canterbury with the words 'Jesus is coming, look busy' tattooed across his bottom. I thought this would be a great phrase to have printed on the wristbands as a conversation starter with light-hearted humour. It was, but not all my Christian friends approved and saw the funny side of it!

Street Pastors are known for giving out flip-flops to ladies who have taken their high heel shoes off when coming out of a pub or club a bit worse for wear. Sometimes, we will walk people home or get them safely into a taxi. One late night in Wimbledon, we met a girl who was distraught about losing her ring that had been given to her by her grandmother. We prayed for it to be found and joined in the search along the high street for about half an hour. She'd given up hope and was about to get into a taxi to go home when we found the ring. You can imagine the joy and relief and tears that followed. As we walked away, she shouted after us, "I love Street Pastors!"

Our presence on the streets stops some things from happening. I've been told by one of the more notorious characters we know in Mitcham that he's not able to do stuff when Street Pastors are around. We are not the police but the church on the streets. Our presence is supposed to be 'light' exposing darkness, and 'salt' adding flavour. We aim to be good news bringing faith, hope and love.

A lot of our team are older ladies. In conversation, Liz may say to a young person, "Pull up your trousers." And they'll say, "Yes auntie." She can get away with that, I couldn't. Our team not only carries compassion but their own life experiences and professional skills. We have nurses, window cleaners, people on benefits, engineers, builders, cleaners, IT workers and so on, all walking the streets.

Daniel was from Romania, and we would often meet him on the streets, where he was homeless and dependant on alcohol. We'd buy him food, sit and talk with him, pray with him and befriend him. He had a soft heart and would sometimes cry. He would come to our group at the Mission and one Christmas, came to our home with some others for a party. Over many years, different people got involved in his life, and a friend called Martin helped to sort out his paperwork and champion him through the courts for past misdemeanours. Daniel's life began to slowly change. He found a companion who gave him a home and he got weaned off the drink. Daniel attended church and surrendered his life to Jesus and a new day dawned for him. During this time, he would regularly be arrested and placed in detention centres and later released, but his newfound faith kept him strong and hopeful.

Daniel is now himself a Street Pastor and a member of our team. When people who knew him see him, they can't believe the change. He is a living, walking testimony that lives can change, and a better day can come.

I hope Daniel will one day tell his own story and write his own book.

Chapter 38

So, what's the Church Doing in the Community Then?

I was chairing the Churches Together in Mitcham group meeting, and working our way through the agenda, when a lady spoke up. Judy was a local Labour councillor and had been the Mayor of Merton the year before. She sometimes attended St Barnabas Church. Judy was new to our meetings, but wasn't afraid to ask direct questions, like, "So, what's the Church doing in the community then?"

We were mainly church leaders from across denominations: Baptist, Methodist, Anglican, Roman Catholic and free church – that's me! Her question took us all by surprise and started to make me think. As can usually be the case when someone asks a question like that, I became a bit defensive. I thought, "What do you mean? What is the Church doing? We're praying of course…" I am sure we were all doing stuff in the community that Judy knew nothing about, but it stirred in me a restlessness that perhaps more was needed.

Judy's question would provoke me. I took it back to church and began sharing with people. Hayley was particularly passionate about doing something significant and sustainable in the community. At a meeting with Hayley in May 2007, the vision for a community action project was born.

It would be called, The Jeremiah Project, a working project name of All Nations Revival Church, and be influenced by a Bible passage from the book of Jeremiah Chapter 29, where God speaks to his people about "seeking the peace and prosperity of the city where you are".

Our strap line would be from verse 11: "Plans to prosper, give Hope and a future worth having..."

We would research the needs and mobilise Christians from across different churches. Street Pastors was already underway, and our church was now meeting in the school. It felt like time for another adventure.

Judy would become a good friend and join this adventure with us. She trained as a Street Pastor and joined our team. She was a voice for us among her peers in the local authority and supported our money management workshops, becoming a key member of the Hope Bus team. In October 2011, I organised a Holy Land Tour to Israel and Judy joined with her friend, Debbie. I had the joy and honour of baptising Judy as a believer in Jesus Christ in the River Jordan. She has retired now and moved away, but when we meet, I often remind her of that challenging question she asked, "So, what's the Church doing in the community then?"

CHAPTER 39

The Jeremiah Project

The launching of the Jeremiah Project coincided with the promotion and development of the government's Every Child Matters agenda and Extended Schools community offer. Schools were being 'clustered' together locally and encouraged to offer a menu of services to the wider community. I saw this as a strategic opportunity for the Church to get involved.

There were three main areas from our research that we focused on: family support and relationships, drug education, money management and budget coaching. We would use recognised Christian charities to train our people and offer relational support, lessons, coaching, and workshops in these different areas. As a church we were perfectly placed at Cricket Green School and a growing part of their community.

Once, Celia, the Headteacher, asked if the church could help support the mum of one of the boys at school. He had learning difficulties and she was fighting cancer, had limited literacy and was not managing well at home. One of our team members, Kathy, who was a qualified nurse, befriended her. She helped her manage her meds, attended hospital visits with her and assisted with cleaning and shopping. There have been many other times where referrals have been made and we've been able to work together.

I was a governor at school, but also got invited to join the Mitcham Town Schools Cluster as a representative of the community. The group consisted of headteachers from local schools, a dynamic Cluster Co-ordinator called Kristina, me, and Angie from St Mark's Family Centre. I was way out of my depth and comfort zone but couldn't help thinking that I had been positioned by God very deliberately.

Over the years, I have learnt the importance of being in the right place at the right time. Relationships, friendships, vulnerability and trust have grown, and many opportunities for partnership work have come out of it. People have come and gone, but I feel honoured to still be there. The group is now called Mitcham Town Community Trust and the Jeremiah Project remains a member. I came to realise the pressure headteachers were under, and from time to time would organise a get-together at the local Toby Carvery. This was an opportunity for everyone to socialise, share informally and for me and others to offer pastoral support and encouragement. They may have only come to humour me, but it was fun anyway!

Love Mitcham is another campaign of the Jeremiah Project. It's emblazoned on the Hope Bus and a message we promote among all we meet. In association with Merton Street Pastors, we give out wristbands that 'big up' our town. Some people say Mitcham is not a nice place. I disagree. I always tell people it's an amazing place because they're in Mitcham, and they make a difference! The young people love the wristbands and collect the different colours.

There's a regular in the White Lion of Mortimer pub who also collects them, and I joke that he's got a business selling them on. We did a big Love Mitcham event in the centre of Mitcham in May 2011 over two days. Our newly-converted Hope Bus was there and we had stalls, food and fun things for the children to do. The main event was the dramatised production of The Cross and the Switchblade, performed by the Lantern Arts Theatre Company in a marquee. The weather was wet and windy, but the tent was full, and we even managed to pull it off without getting arrested! I read this story when I first became a Christian and it had a big impact on my life. I still cry when I watch the film, even though it's so dated.

We were commissioned by Merton to run an eighteen-month Healthy Schools project among the Mitcham cluster schools in 2014. Hayley took the lead on this and did a great job. Elaine, a NHS Schools Nurse, trained as a volunteer Parish Nurse to work with us in the community. She led a team in Hall Place among those in temporary housing offering blood pressure checks, healthy eating advice, a listening ear and prayer. Kim was employed as a part-time co-ordinator for the Jeremiah Project, and helped us achieve the Queen's Award for Voluntary Service in 2014. The same year, Merton Street Pastors also won it! We were invited to send four of our volunteers to Buckingham Palace for a garden party with the Queen. Jane was one of them.

As Harry Hill would say, "What are the chances of that?"

KEVIN VICKERS

Chapter 40

Hope Bus Stories

Where do you park a double-decker bus? This was one of my nightmares! I needed somewhere accessible, local and secure. Outside my house was not an option, but I had secretly spied the vicarage in Locks Lane, where my friend, the Rev Steve, of St Mark's Church lived. Steve already had a relationship with the Hope Bus, a year earlier he had spent 24 hours on the back seat! But would his wife Rebecca agree?

Steve and Rebecca did agree to house the Hope Bus in their front garden temporarily until I could find a more permanent home. I never did. It wasn't until they moved out two years later, that I had to relocate the bus because the Church of England said it wouldn't be fair for the new vicar to find a double-decker bus parked in his driveway. Rebecca would say that if you stood on the upper deck, you could see directly into their bedroom. Apparently, the bus would also obscure the sunlight from their front windows. They were so gracious! When they moved to St Mark's Church Kennington, I presented them with a black and white photograph of the Hope Bus as a fond reminder of their time with us.

I wrote this scripture on the picture:

"He will watch over your life; the LORD will watch over your coming and going both now and forevermore"

Psalm 121:7-8 (NIV)

The new vicar, the Rev Nigel, became my friend, too. He would become part of the Hope Bus team, but by then we had secured a new home at the back of Cricket Green School.

I had a love/hate relationship driving the bus. It would scare the life out of me and keep me awake at nights thinking about it. There was always so much that could go wrong. The battery could be flat, the lights might not work, there could be a car blocking our exit or a hazard in the way.

I once drove to St Cecilia's Primary School, in Cheam, for an ARK project. We wouldn't normally take it out of Merton, but a friend had asked nicely so we agreed as a one off. I'd clearly communicated to the school our time of arrival but when we got there the gates were closed and I was on the main road with traffic behind me. I pulled the bus up onto the pavement to let the traffic pass and then, with a bit of help, had to reverse along a main road to turn into the school, where the caretaker eventually opened the gates. At Merton Abbey School we took a chance and drove it back the wrong way along a one-way street because there was no way we could go straight on! We've had to saw branches off trees, remove posts from the ground, and in one school, we left a bit of an oil leak in the playground. I have generally enjoyed the driving and loved the feeling of returning home safely after a completed project, parking and switching off the engine. *Gobsmacked!*

We were in a school once, and the Rev John, from Mitcham Parish Church, was on our team that day.

He was upstairs with a class and supposed to be telling the story of the 'feeding of the five thousand'. I was downstairs with some others listening, and heard him graphically talking about the head of John the Baptist being cut off and placed on a platter. Eventually, he got round to the right story, and I learnt for the first time the context of the feeding of the five thousand!

In another school, one of our team needed a bread roll as a visual aid and found one that had been thrown away in the bin. Later, Father Peter, the Roman Catholic priest, joined our team and was telling the same story with another class. To our horror, he picked up the bread roll, broke some off and gave it to the children to eat before we could stop him! Rev Steve was teaching the story once and had brought fish fingers with him. Those that know me will know that I'm often picking crumbs off the floor when I see them and tidying up around me. Steve began to break up the fish fingers and pass them around the children, pieces falling everywhere. I was upstairs at the back of the bus, behind the class, and all the helpers turned immediately to look at the expression on my face!

It was in preparing for an Acts of Random Kindness Project that Mum received some news that she'd waited thirty years to hear. When Dad died, Mum had tried to find out if he had been alone or if there was anyone with him on the platform at the Underground station. It was after church one Sunday morning, and Mum, with some others, had stayed behind to make and bake the fish-shaped biscuits that we would be giving to the children the following day.

They were in the Food Tech Room at Cricket Green School, and Mum was getting to know a new couple, Sid and Maureen, who had recently joined us from another church. In the conversation, Mum happened to say that her husband had been a postman working at a sorting office in London. She told them that he had had a heart attack on the platform of Colliers Wood Station some thirty years ago at 5:30 am in the morning. Sid looked up and replied, "I was with him."

Mum's prayer had been answered!

Chapter 41
Mayor's Chaplain

Nick has been the longest-serving governor on the governing body at Cricket Green School and has been my Vice Chair for sixteen years. He is far more qualified to do the job that I do, but has humbly shown me nothing but support and encouragement.

In May 2009, he was elected Mayor of the London Borough of Merton and asked me to be his Chaplain. I was honoured; a bit scared but also excited about what was to come. I got to pray at the opening of council meetings, attend functions with the Mayor and, on formal occasions, wear a big silver cross around my neck. I think it made me look like an Anglican vicar.

Nick was a great Mayor, but a bit unconventional. He played his guitar at the Mayor Making Ceremony and sometimes went off script. I loved it! He held a Mayor's reception in his parlour soon after he was elected. It was a formal do, with senior local authority officers, other dignitaries and me and Jane. We enjoyed the occasion, met great people, did some small talk, and got to know and appreciate Carl the Mayor's Attendant. Mayor's come and go annually, but Carl has remained over many years. He is the one constant, upholding his office with dignity and respect.

Then, I spotted her out of the corner of my eye! The lady from the Outside Events Department.

It had been six years since I'd met her with Mike, and that hadn't turned out to be the best of meetings.

I was sure it had been her who instigated the injunction against us when I was playing Jesus. Nick knew nothing of my past misdemeanours and was about to do one of the worst things ever.

Suddenly, he called her over. I could tell she recognised me. Inside I was screaming, "NO! Please don't do it!" He introduced us, and I heard myself say, "We have already met". Turning to the lady from the Outside Events Department, Nick declared, "This is Kevin. His church is doing amazing things in the community." Nick then walked away leaving the two of us standing together, not knowing what to say to each other. I can laugh now, and I love telling the story, but it was like out of a comedy sketch. We smiled awkwardly for a bit before excusing ourselves.

That same year, a month earlier, I received a civic community award and had to attend a ceremony in the council chambers. Things had miraculously turned around and we no longer felt like the 'naughty church' in Mitcham. Even though, somewhere, filed away in the council archives, was a piece of paper serving an injunction on Jesus and the devil!

Did I read somewhere that there is a redeemer?

Chapter 42
Speaking "Mitcham"

When the Christian Church first started, there were Jews from countries all over the Roman Empire visiting Jerusalem. Most of them would have known Greek, but they also spoke their local language, too. Jesus's local language was Aramaic. The birth of the Church was supernatural, and when the Holy Spirit was poured out on the early disciples, they immediately started to raise their voices in praise to God using other tongues. It just so happened that the crowd who gathered recognised those tongues as their own native languages.

This is what it says:

"We hear them declaring the wonders of God in our own tongues...what does this mean?"

Acts 2:11-12 (NIV)

I believe it means that God wants to communicate to all of us in a way that we can understand.

In **Psalm 19:1-4**, David writes:

"The heavens declare the glory of God; the skies proclaim the work of his hands. Day after day they pour forth speech; night after night they display knowledge. There is no speech or language where their voice is not heard. Their voice goes out into all the earth, their words to the ends of the world"

Recently, I decided to keep the children in the main meeting and not send them to their Sunday school classes. I felt the need to talk to everyone and knew that it would be a challenge to keep everyone's attention. I had prepared a sermon, but that would not do, I needed to think on my feet. I invited all the children to the front including mums with babies. We sang, 'He's Got the Whole World in His Hands' and I kept adding verses about little babies, you, and me brother/sister, all our troubles, and finally, "He's got all our futures in his hands!" There was something there for everyone and I could see that the adults were getting something from this, too. My sermon was to be about David, a man after God's heart. I also did some drama! I got a brother chasing his sister across the hall and told everyone that God loves it when we chase after him. I was doing my best to communicate to everyone in a way they could understand. *And this is my passion in my town of Mitcham and wherever I find myself.*

God is best at doing this, but sometimes the Church is the worst. God sent Jesus to be like us, speak our language and wear our clothes. We get to know what God is really like when we read about Jesus. Most people think they know about Jesus because they look at the Church. Sadly, that's where the communication sometimes breaks down.

An older translation of the Bible says of Jesus:

"And the common people heard him gladly."

Mark 12:37 (AKJV)

That's not a patronising statement, it's fact! The everyday man in the street warmed to him. One of the greatest compliments you can give me is to tell me that I've made something simple to understand; accessible, relevant and religious jargon free.

I did some stuff on Facebook live recently that was deliberately provocative. Not in a rude way, but in a way that would make people think. I called that *Gobsmacked,* too! But it wasn't about me, it was about Jesus. I know some of my Facebook friends watch the short videos, even though they don't 'like' or comment. I hope what I do will speak their language.

These are some of the titles:

- "Good people don't go to heaven."
- "I thought the sun only shone on the righteous."
- "He did what to the fat cow?"

I can only speak one language, and not very well. I have a limited vocabulary and sometimes Jane helps me finish my sentences. But I don't care. Like Paul in the Bible, I can say,

> *"But by the grace of God I am what I am, and his grace to me was not without effect."*
> **1 Corinthians Chapter 15:10 NIV**

I've discovered that everything is possible and life is full of opportunities, if we're prepared to step out and have a go!

The last section of this book is about some of my adventures: *Having a go!*

KEVIN VICKERS

GOBSMACKED

ON MISSIONS AND ADVENTURES

KEVIN VICKERS

Chapter 43
The Blind Leading the Blind

Once a year, for about thirteen years, I would go on holiday with my blind and visually-impaired friends to The Torch Holiday and Retreat Centre in Hurstpierpoint, West Sussex. This was one of my annual highlights, made even more special by working with Gail, the visionary and crazy Centre Manager, who became one of my best mates. I was there to lead the spiritual devotions every day, but got to enjoy the week or ten days holiday as much as everyone else. There were no limits to what we would do. Except when the insurance company refused to insure blind people jumping out of an aeroplane – *Gobsmacked!*

Early on, Gareth, who is registered blind, taught me how to use my new iPhone when we sat in deckchairs on Brighton Pier. He showed me how to put the phone into 'Accessibility' mode, which totally changes how it works. I thought it would be funny to do this with Judy's phone, once, without her knowing. The trouble was, we couldn't get it back to normal and the whole thing backfired on me! I had the joy of baptising Gareth in the sea when he courageously overcame his fear of going under the water. We nicknamed him The Tupperware Man – because of a funny poem he loved to share at the end of holiday concert.

Gail would organise a packed programme of activities. We'd do things such as go-karting, horse riding, canoeing, abseiling, tennis, cycling, crate building, and 4x4 off-road driving, to mention a few.

Once, we were canoeing on a reservoir when one of the canoes capsized. Those of us who were guiding got into the water to help people to safety without realising we'd left Carol behind. There she was, bobbing up and down in the water. All was well, and we all laughed about it later. Dave is registered blind, and one time we rode a tandem together. I was steering – we crashed but lived to tell the tale.

The week would be full of water fights, where Gail and I would always come off the worst. We would muck about like brother and sister, and once I threw her into a dirty, filthy lake, near to where we were having a picnic. Gail is quite a well-built lady, and an elderly couple picnicking nearby gave her a little hand towel to dry herself. On another occasion, we'd hired rowing boats on a river. I thought it would be funny to moor up by a cow's field and using my paddle to throw a cow pat at Gail as she went past in her boat. I didn't realise that it was soft until it splattered all over her, and then I knew I'd gone too far!

Sometimes, I would take Bible college students with me, so that they could serve. Like me over the years, they would learn so much from our blind and visually-impaired friends.

Both Will and Philippa have no sight. They met on one of the holidays, fell in love, got married and have three beautiful sighted daughters. I was honoured to be invited, and attended their wedding.

Philippa told me once, that she did not want to be prayed for to see. She said that when her eyes are opened in Heaven, the first person she wants to see is Jesus. Anyone or anything else would be an anti-climax! Philippa has a beautiful voice and Will is a gifted pianist.

One year, Simon came, and made it clear to everyone that he was there for the activities and not the religious bit. In fact, every evening when I did my talks, Simon went to the pub on his own. One night it was late, and he hadn't returned, so me and Dave, a friend of Gail's, went to look for him. We found him quite drunk, propping up the bar at the Horse Inn. It was interesting guiding a blind drunk man back to the centre, but we managed. Simon kept coming to the holiday, and one night he didn't go to the pub but stayed for my talk for the first time. He had begun to share and open up and was touched by the love of God evident among us. That week, Simon became a Christian, and the transformation of his heart and life since then has been remarkable. He would still go to the pub but not usually when I was doing my talks!

I learnt to treat my blind and visually-impaired friends the same as I would treat people with sight. They didn't want special treatment but to be listened to and respected. I'd get to appreciate their fears and anxieties and be amazed at how they joked about their disabilities. One of their favourite things to do was the 'Nightline' at Blackland's Farm Activity Centre. The sighted people would be blindfolded and those without sight would lead and guide us around an obstacle course following a rope line. It was the blind leading the blind!

Although the centre has since closed, I am still in contact with many of my 'holiday friends' through social media, and some of them access things my church does online. Gail and her husband, Stuart, still live in the village and have a massive heart for people and a gift for hospitality. During August 2021, they invited the whole Vickers family (nine adults and three children) to stay in their new house while they went away on holiday for two weeks.

She's still a great friend, even though I threw a cow pat at her!

Chapter 44

A Goat and a Chicken in Sierra Leone

My first visit to Sierra Leone in West Africa was in April 2001, nine months before the civil war was officially declared over. I travelled with James, who was from there and had become a member of the Mission. His story had endeared us and opened the way for us to partner and support his church back home in Wellington, Freetown.

James had come to the UK in August 1994 for a conference but was unable to return home because of the war. His wife, Binty, was pregnant with their first daughter, Abigail. She had fled to Guinea and then Senegal, and with a little help from us, was eventually reunited with James on the 9th March, 2000 at Heathrow Airport. The whole church turned out with banners and flowers, and the story was covered by our local 'Guardian' newspaper. James was very popular at church. People loved him, trusted him and wanted to help him. Once, when our daughter Rachel was about ten, he took her and three of her friends from church to the Harvester restaurant for some food. Apparently, they got some funny looks but had a great time. My children grew up with an 'Uncle James' in their lives.

We flew via The Gambia, but our connecting flight was cancelled, so we stayed three days in a holiday resort that seemed to have been dropped into an area surrounded by extreme poverty. It was a bizarre experience, and it felt so wrong that we were there. I got to try their famous 'Wonjo juice', though and visited Kachikally Crocodile Pool. There were crocodiles everywhere, and a man with a stick would walk in front of us as our protector!

When we arrived in Sierra Leone, we had to get from Lungi Airport – which is on an island – to Freetown, on the mainland. There appeared to be only one way: the massively overcrowded ferry. I would find out later there were other ways, if you could afford it, and one of them was a rickety old helicopter. The quickest, but not necessarily the safest! We would chance the helicopter on the way home. There were few white people about then, so I was very noticeable and a bit naïve. But James would look after me.

Freetown was full of thousands of displaced people who had sought refuge in the city from the civil war. They were living in makeshift shelters in displacement camps set up by the government. We visited an amputee camp and were heartbroken to see small children with missing limbs. James recalled later how he wept from the heart as he watched a little boy creep out of his shelter, with both hands having been cut near the elbows. Ever since then he has wanted to champion the cause of the voiceless.

I found myself in another world that I had no idea existed. I was totally outside of my comfort zone and overwhelmed by what I saw. We visited James's church, the True Gospel Harvest Mission, and met Pastor Daniel, Pastor Moses and Pastor Alieu. They honoured me with the little that they had. The Mission had recently sent a container filled with all sorts of things they would use. We had watched a video of them unpacking it at the dock with joy and singing. It was now so good to meet them all face to face.

They organised 'Revival' meetings for me to preach at with translation. I have no idea what the translation was like! We took a trip through the bush to the provinces, where we held additional meetings, and I preached to large gatherings. It took hours and hours to get anywhere. I think we had up to ten tyre changes on the car I travelled in. Someone would disappear into the bush in the remotest of places and come back with another part-worn tyre and off we'd go again. When the children saw me looking out of the car window, they would wave and call after me, 'Pumui', which means white man. James told me that they were happy because my being there was a sign that the war was over and that it was safe again.

I would return to Sierra Leone four more times. I took my eldest son, Sam, in 2006, and he celebrated his eighteenth birthday riding a motorbike for the first time. The pastors stopped a random guy, gave him some money, and we borrowed his bike for an hour. Sam had a great time riding around a dirt football pitch, taking his mind off the masses of mosquito bites he was suffering from.

On leaving the country, Sam was being bribed to hand over money at the passport desk until I angrily intervened and they let him go. Another time, I went with Paul Keeys, the son of Cliff, who had originally introduced me to Walk Through the Bible. Paul was now in charge, but I didn't really know him when we met up at Heathrow Airport in October 2007.

We were going to train thirty leaders to teach the Walk Through the Bible programme in their context. My pastor friends were hosting the training and we would provide the materials and train them to teach the lessons. It was an amazing time, full of laughter, special memories, and me and Paul got on really well. We had one mosquito net between us, so we had to push our beds together to make it work!

During my visits, I came to appreciate another culture by living in it for a while. I made it clear from the beginning that it was not just financial support that we wanted to give, but as a church we wanted to share our lives and become their friends too. I've been welcomed into people's homes, shared blessings from the scriptures and tried to help them resolve conflicts amongst each other. It has been a privilege.

My final story is in 2010, when James and I visited Bumban Village, where he was born. I met his dad and Father Franco, the Roman Catholic priest who had taken him to school as a young boy. Of all his many brothers, James is the only one who went to school.

Bond Primary School in Mitcham had prepared a video and provided resources and gifts for us to take to the village as part of an international support project. The whole village came out to meet us as we arrived along the dirt road. They sang and danced, and the village elders welcomed us formally at a reception with speeches and prayers. Then they gave me a gift of a live goat and a chicken. I was unsure what to do and was praying inside that they were not expecting me to kill the goat! They weren't, not there and then, anyway.

It was a wonderful occasion, and they had been incredibly generous in honouring us. We visited the new village school and presented them with the lovely resources and gifts from Bond Primary School. Afterwards, I travelled the long journey back to Freetown in the back of a pickup truck with a goat and a chicken for company.

KEVIN VICKERS

Chapter 45
History Makers

Rob Frost used to be the vicar of Mitcham Methodist Church when I was in my early twenties. He was the cool, young vicar running the Rob Frost Road Show, attempting to make Christianity relevant to the younger generation. He went on to found Share Jesus International, aimed at training and mobilising individuals and churches for missions.

In 2004, Rob invited me to attend a leadership training programme called ILI at Cliff College Derbyshire. ILI stands for the International Leadership Institute, which is based in Atlanta, Georgia, USA. Rob was one of the founding team members. Its aim is to train and equip leaders in eight core values of the Christian faith, and today has alumni all over the world. I loved the training and could see how each core value unpacked would inform every part of my life, faith and work. Afterwards, I sent an email to Rob, thanking him for the invitation and offering any pastoral support I could give to his future trips. He invited me to go to Hungary with him to teach the following year.

I was part of a small team. Oliver would come from Austria and Judit would be our translator. There were very few people on the programme – less than ten – but that didn't seem to matter. Rob was well known in Christian circles and was a popular platform speaker and broadcaster to hundreds, sometimes thousands, of people.

I was impressed with his humility in being prepared to travel all that way for so few. I have learnt from Rob's example and aim to be like him. We were next to Lake Balaton, the largest lake in Central Europe, and one of the region's foremost tourist destinations. During a break time on a very hot day, I have a funny memory of both of us standing in the lake in our pants – because we never had our swimming costumes with us. Rob had the gift of making people feel that they were important and would give them his undivided attention. He believed in personal mentoring and invested in the next generation. He would encourage me to do the same.

I was invited to be part of his team to Romania in November 2006. We would be training students at the Partium Christian University in Oradea. Wow! And I didn't even have an A Level, let alone a degree. I was one of the many people Rob Frost mentored before his untimely death in November 2007. I miss our occasional breakfasts in Raynes Park, but just like Mr Pavitt when I was a boy, I will always be grateful for Rob's time and investment in my later life. If it were not for his encouragement, I would never have gotten involved with the International Leadership Institute. Writing this book has helped me see, more clearly than ever, how one thing leads to the next.

The Hungarian trip opened the door for Jane and I to return the following year with four of our youth group. We worked with a Baptist Pastor, called Zsolty, in Kondorus. We'd never done anything like that before, but our young people were great. We were cared for, ate well and everyone had opportunities to share and experience life in a different culture. Louise celebrated her eighteenth birthday and was embarrassingly serenaded by a man with a violin in a restaurant!

Zsolty was well built and very tall, but when you pronounce his name in English it sounds like Shorty. He visited us in the UK once for a holiday, and we hosted him and showed him around the London sights. One day at church, I was praying for him with a group of others, saying his name, Zsolty, and the more I said it, the more I thought, "But you're not a shorty, you're a tally." I sensed other people in the circle were thinking the same, but the harder I tried not to say it, the more I kept saying his name. I was trying to hold it together and pray whilst Jane was shaking with silent laughter. A ridiculous situation!

Mark and Joanna were part of Rob's team and were responsible for developing the ILI training material for young and emerging leaders in Europe. This stream was called History Makers Journey and would also be built around the eight core values, with an extra focus on the practice of spiritual disciplines. I got to travel and teach with them in Austria, Czech Republic and Romania, and had the joy of marrying them on 4th July, 2009. It was on these missions that I would get to meet and serve with Martin, who would take over from Mark and Joanna and become the European Director for History Makers.

Martin would become a best friend, and we would go on many adventures together throughout Europe – making history!

KEVIN VICKERS

Chapter 46
Polish Pranks

I was teaching a session on biblical leadership at a Catholic Retreat Centre in Poland, run by our friend and colleague, Priest Jurek. I was giving examples of great Christian leaders, when I mentioned the great reformer Martin Luther. My friend, Martin, was sitting at the back of the room working on his laptop, but at that moment his head shot up and immediately caught my attention. It wasn't until after I'd finished my session that I realised that siting the great Martin Luther in a Roman Catholic setting may not have been the best example to use. Martin and I (not Martin Luther) were sharing a room once in Poland and he had to leave early. After he'd gone, I found a Playmobil figure of Martin Luther in my bedside cabinet. I keep it on my shelf at home to remind me of that infamous quote!

I took Wesley, who's from Ghana and from my church to a History Makers Journey in Poland in September 2011. Martin was there too. When someone else was teaching, Martin and I slipped out and managed to find a key to Wesley's room. Well, we thought it was Wesley's room, but it turned out to be someone else's! After locking it up we managed to get into Wesley's room.

Outside, in a cupboard, I found a large, red cape with a hood and white beard, probably Father Christmas's. I coaxed Martin to put it on and, using Wesley's camera, I photographed him creeping about in the room.

We also lifted Wesley's bed and put it on top of another bed in his room. Wesley had been taking lots of photos on his camera to document our group's time together. We transferred one of the pictures I had taken of Martin, and made it his screen saver on Wesley's laptop and called it, The Mystery Intruder. We locked the room, Martin got changed and we slipped back into the session. At the end of the meeting, the leader stood up and asked if people would let him have any photographs they'd taken, for an album he was compiling. Wesley went to get his camera and me and Martin looked at one another in horror and quickly went after him! We laughed and laughed, with Wesley later and deleted the Mystery Intruder photographs from his camera.

It wasn't only in Poland that crazy things happened. We were in Spain once running a History Makers, in what seemed like a convent. We were hiring the buildings that contained beautiful gardens with fruit trees and a tall water tower with a stork's nest at the top. When no-one was about, I challenged Martin to climb the metal ladder to the stork's nest and check it out. It was empty, but we did find a one-eyed cat in the garden. We made a Union Jack flag, wrote, "Kevin and Martin and the one-eyed cat was here." Martin then climbed up and put it in the stork's nest. Inside the building, there was a bust of the Pope holding a wooden dove. If you look carefully at the group photographs taken at the end of our History Makers Journey, you may be able to see a dove on my shoulder, with Martin standing behind me. Jane says that when Martin and I get together we can be like two naughty schoolboys.

I was teaching on visionary leadership in Albania, on the roof of Ina's mum and dad's home, close to the beach near Tirana. My Bible was open at the book of Nehemiah and the page was slightly torn. A gust of wind tore a small part of the page out and I never saw it again. A bit later, I was in Ukraine and between sessions, I was talking to Alena. She was sharing with me and crying a bit. I told her I had a scripture for her. I turned to the book of Nehemiah, Chapter 2 and when I looked for the verse it wasn't there. "Oh no." I said, "The devil's stolen your scripture!" We laughed and I continued to share with her.

Although I joke about, I take what I do very seriously, particularly when it affects others. I sometimes get it wrong and can go too far. But I also look for the joy and laughter, the fun and craziness that can lift spirits, warm hearts, and create lifelong memories. I hope you can too.

As **Proverbs 17:22** says,

> *"A cheerful heart is good medicine."*

KEVIN VICKERS

Chapter 47
More European Exploits

It has been a rich experience meeting new people in different countries. Sometimes, I get to serve with familiar faces, such as Chris and Roderick, who are both Chick-fil-A operators in the USA. I love listening to them teach on servant leadership, using their own business model as an excellent practical example. Chris teaches mobilisation by mobilising the group to act out Nehemiah, leading the people to rebuild the walls around Jerusalem. He directs the acting and makes it into a film which we watch later.

The Chick-fil-A slogan is, 'Eat mor Chikin'. I once took a photograph of them with Mike, another operator, standing outside a McDonald's in Lithuania holding menus adverting hamburgers! There's always friendly banter and a bit of competition going on between the brits and the Americans! I travelled for hours in the back of a car with Adam, the worship pastor at a church in Auburn Alabama. We were singing old songs, hymns and choruses at the top of our lungs as we made our way to the conference venue in Georgia (Europe).

Sometimes, the laughs are on me. Such as the time I was in Albania, and we'd taken a bus into the capital city of Tirana for some sightseeing. At the end of the day, we were running for the bus, and I fell down the biggest pothole ever. I disappeared up to my neck in a hole and was fortunate not to be seriously hurt. Martin and the others saw me vanish and when they realised I was still alive, they laughed their heads off.

They helped me out and we carried on running for the bus. Then, I did the exact same thing and fell down another pothole. I think it is true to say that their concern for me at that moment was trumped by their inability to hold it together. They will not let me forget that!

Another time, I joined the team in Ukraine a day after Martin and the others had arrived. We were staying in a large house, close to the conference centre. It was dark and late when I got there. Martin had a key and said that the man in the house was a bit 'moany' and we needed to be very quiet when we came in. We got to the front door, and I thought the switch was for a light, so I pushed it – and the loudest bell rang and probably woke the rest of the street. The man we were trying to avoid opened the front door wearing his pants, and not a lot more. We made our apologies and crept up the stairs trying hard not to laugh.

One of the first adventures I had was travelling with Martin and Joanna from Austria to the Czech Republic by train. We were doing back-to-back History Maker Journeys. In Austria, we had stayed in the most beautiful newly-built wooden apartments close to the mountains, and I had fortuitously been allocated a whole floor, fully furnished and all to myself. The view was spectacular. I found out that Martin and Joanna had nothing like the luxury or view that I enjoyed! An overnight sleeper train had been booked for our travel to the Czech Republic by our host in Austria. We boarded the train and found our sleeper carriage. Martin had the top bunk and climbed the ladder. He reached into the bed, only to find a lady already sleeping there.

In fact, the whole carriage was occupied with sleeping people.

We crept out and discovered later that our host had booked us for daytime rather than night-time on the train. The guard graciously allowed us to travel in the seating carriage. In the Czech Republic, we would stay at a purpose-built Christian holiday and conference centre called Malenovice. We were allocated our rooms and later had food together. I was telling Martin and Joanna how amazing it was to have jacuzzis in our rooms and so much space. They thought I was messing about. As it turned out, I was the only one who had a suite with a jacuzzi – their rooms were quite basic!

I have had the trusted privilege as a protestant Christian of being invited five times to speak and teach both History Makers and Walk Through the Bible at a Roman Catholic annual retreat centre in Poland. I have skied twice in Georgia, broken my leg playing basketball in the Czech Republic and preached a sermon in a Baptist church in Moscow.

I am continually overwhelmed – actually, *Gobsmacked* at the opportunities God has opened up for me. Whoever said being a Christian is boring?

I feel like David when he prayed,

> *"Who am I, O Sovereign LORD, and what is my family, that you have brought me this far?"*
>
> **2 Samuel 7:18 (NIV)**

KEVIN VICKERS

Chapter 48
Israeli Adventures

When I ran the youth group at church, I borrowed a minibus and organised a poor man's 'holy land' tour. Over the course of a few days, we did things such as eat fish paste sandwiches on Streatham Common, ascend a hill in Norwood, to talk about the temptations of Jesus, and I pretended to baptise John Nye in the dirty River Wandle. I wanted the young people to experience the Bible coming to life.

I first went to Israel with Jane when she was seven-and-a-half months pregnant, carrying our son, Samuel. He was nearly born there! It's not a holiday, but a Holy Land tour, walking in the footsteps of Jesus and getting to see and appreciate the Bible lands, the people and the culture. I have been back a few times, and in association with Walk Through the Bible Ministries and Maranatha Tours, I have had the joy of helping to lead tours and taking people from church.

The Bible really does come to life when you are in Israel. We would stop and pause at a particular place and read a passage from the Bible, allowing God to bring the words alive in our hearts and minds. Sometimes, I would re-enact the story with them. We visited Lazarus's tomb in Bethany, where Jesus had raised him from the dead four days after he'd died. I borrowed a toilet roll from the hotel and used it to wrap Ben up like a mummy and put him in the tomb. I stood outside with our tour group and retold the story.

When I shouted, "Lazarus come out," Ben hobbled out of the tomb to our shouts and cheers. We got some dirty looks from a more orthodox group standing nearby! Ben played the dead person at the village of Nain, too. This time I borrowed a hammock from the hotel and used it like a stretcher that was carried by four people. I retold the story of the widow of Nain, whose son had died, and how Jesus interrupted the funeral to bring him back to life.

We visited Cana in Galilee, where Jesus had attended a wedding and turned the water into wine. Sid and Maureen asked me if I would lead them in renewing their marriage vows. I presented them with a certificate and prayed a blessing over their lives and future together. That was very special. I bought some wine in Cana once, thinking that if this was the place where Jesus turned the bath water into the 'champagne' of all red wine, then I wanted some. It tasted disgusting. I was livid! How dare they sell such horrible wine at such a significant place!

Sid, who is quite small in height, came up to me as we were about to go through the gate into Capernaum. He said, "I'm not allowed in," pointing to the sign on the gate that said, "No shorts".

I also bought a sling like David would have used to confront Goliath. I take it to schools when I'm teaching the children. We always visit the Wailing Wall in Jerusalem, where some people write their prayers on small pieces of paper and place them in the cracks in the wall. One of my favourite places is Nazareth Village, an area that has been reconstructed to look as it would have done at the time of Jesus.

It brought a lump to my throat and a tear to my eye to watch the carpenter at work. He was chopping wood when a splinter flew off and he pretended it caught him in the eye. As we stood and watched, he quoted Jesus, who said:

> *"Why do you look at the speck of sawdust in your brother's eye and pay no attention to the plank in your own eye?"*
>
> **Matthew 7:3 (NIV)**

Suddenly, I understood the context in which Jesus had been teaching, and that scripture came alive to me in a new way. I made a conscious note in my mind that that is the way I would teach, too.

I have loved floating in the Dead Sea, meditating in the Garden of Gethsemane and baptising people, such as Judy, in the River Jordan. I've watched the sun rise over the Sea of Galilee, rode a camel into the desert and walked the top of the wall around Jerusalem. I've been able to do and see so much with great people.

I have a photograph of our group standing outside the Garden Tomb in Jerusalem. In the picture we're all saying, "He's not here!" And thank God he's not! The tomb is empty, Jesus is risen and there's hope for the world because of him. At All Nations Revival Church, we sometimes raise our voices in worship and sing:

"Because he lives, I can face tomorrow,

Because he lives all fear is gone,

Because I know, he holds the future,

And life is worth the living just because he lives."

Because He Lives lyrics © Warner/Chappell Edicoes Musicais Ltda, Gaither Music Co., Gaither Music Co. Inc., Hanna Street Music

Chapter 49

Conclusion - Missionary at Home in Mitcham

As you can tell, I love travelling and I love adventures. But I also love coming back home to Mitcham. I know that Mitcham is the place God wants me to live and work out my faith, consistently and faithfully. Sometimes it's harder to do that where you live, and where people know you — even Jesus said that where he grew up.

Hayley loves telling the story of the widow of Nain, a place in Galilee that is only mentioned once in the Bible. Jesus was arriving at the town with a large crowd at the time a funeral procession was leaving. Despair met hope at the gate. Darkness met light and sadness turned to joy when Jesus raised the widow's son and gave him back to his mother. I too, want to interrupt the funeral marches in people's lives in my town of Mitcham, one person at a time through the opportunities I have.

Sarah, from Herrnhut in Germany, was on placement at our church during 2011. Later when she returned home, she sent me a postcard that read:

"Bloom where you are planted"
Mary Engelbreit

It was a powerful statement for me then, and still is. That's what I intend to keep on doing – in the good times and the bad; when I'm happy and when I'm sad, when I feel like it and when I don't. I have learnt that character is built through adversity, and that in the darkest and hardest times, there is potential for the greatest good and most significant transformation to happen. I believe it when the Bible says that, ultimately, it is God who gives us life, and that he has determined the times set for us, and the exact places where we should live. I profoundly realise that, like you, I am alive for such a time as this. I can make a difference, you can make a difference, we can make a difference.

A young camel was talking to his father, "Dad, why is it that we have humps on our back?." His dad replied, "Well, son, in the desert we have to walk long distances and we carry water in our humps to sustain us." The young camel thought about this reply and asked, "What about our legs, dad? Why do we have such long legs and big feet?" "Well, son," said his dad, "it's because in the desert our legs need to be strong to support us, and our feet help keep our balance when walking on the sand." The young camel thought about this and asked, "What about our eyelashes, dad? Why are they so long?" The older camel sighed, and said, "Well, son, in the desert there are sometimes sandstorms. The wind blows the sand up into the air and our eyelashes help protect our eyes from the sand." After a few moments of silence, the young camel asked his dad a final question, "So, dad, why are we in the zoo?"

Like those camels, we're at our best when we are in the place God has called us to be, doing the stuff God has called us to do. And doing it with Him.

My hope in writing this book is that you, too, will be **Gobsmacked** at your own life journey and see things in a fresh new way. May you see how one thing leads to another, and how God promises that in all things he will work for the good of those who love him.

Enjoy the journey!

'Bloom where you are planted.'

KEVIN VICKERS

About the Author

Kevin has been married to Jane for 36 years. They have three adult children, Samuel, Rachel, and Jonathan, three grandchildren Nathan, Lilah, and Elijah, and one more on the way! Kevin has lived in Mitcham all his life, has a background in banking and is the Pastor of All Nations Revival Church. He loves people, teaching, crazy adventures, and fishing, and has a passion for communicating his faith in Jesus in the language of ordinary people.

Printed in Great Britain
by Amazon